Chamb
Itali
Grammar

Chambers

CHAMBERS

An imprint of Chambers Harrap Publishers Ltd
7 Hopetoun Crescent, Edinburgh, EH7 4AY

Chambers Harrap is an Hachette UK company

© Chambers Harrap Publishers Ltd 2009

Chambers® is a registered trademark of Chambers Harrap Publishers Ltd

This third edition published by Chambers Harrap Publishers Ltd 2009
First published as *Harrap's Italian Grammar* in 1990
Second edition published 2002

The moral rights of the author have been asserted
Database right Chambers Harrap Publishers Ltd (makers)

A CIP catalogue record for this book is available from the British Library.

ISBN 978 0550 10509 7

10 9 8 7 6 5 4 3 2 1

Project Editors: Alex Hepworth, Kate Nicholson
With Helen Bleck

www.chambers.co.uk

Designed by Chambers Harrap Publishers Ltd, Edinburgh
Typeset in Rotis Serif and Meta Plus by Macmillan Publishing Solutions
Printed and bound in Spain by Graphy Cems

Contents

CONTENTS

INTRODUCTION

This Italian grammar has been written to meet the needs of all students of Italian, and is particularly useful for those taking school examinations. The essential rules of the Italian language have been explained in terms that are as accessible as possible to all users. Where technical terms have been used then full explanations of these terms have also been supplied. There is also a glossary of grammatical terms on pages 7-14. While literary aspects of the language have not been ignored, the emphasis has been placed squarely on modern spoken Italian. This grammar, with its wealth of lively and typical illustrations of usage taken from the present-day language, is the ideal study tool for all levels – from the beginner who is starting to get to grips with the Italian language through to the advanced user who requires a comprehensive and readily accessible work of reference.

For this new edition the text has been fully revised and updated, while the smart new two-colour design makes consultation even easier and more enjoyable.

Abbreviations used in the text:

fem	feminine
masc	masculine
pl	plural
sing	singular

Note

Italian examples given in the third person may, theoretically, be translated in various ways since, where no pronoun is given, the third person singular and plural may be equivalent to 'he/she/you' and to 'they/you' respectively. In actual usage, of course, context will decide. In this book we have normally translated third person singular examples with 'he/she' and sometimes with 'you' according to the most probable context of utterance.

GLOSSARY OF GRAMMATICAL TERMS

ABSTRACT NOUN An abstract noun is one which refers not to a concrete physical object or a person but to a quality or a concept. Examples of abstract nouns are **happiness, life, length**.

ACTIVE The active form of a verb is the basic form as in I *remember* her. It is normally opposed to the passive form of the verb as in she *will be remembered*.

ADJECTIVAL NOUN An adjectival noun is an adjective used as a noun. For example, the adjective **young** is used as a noun in **the young at heart**.

ADJECTIVE An adjective provides supplementary information about a noun, eg a *small* house, the *Royal* family, an *interesting* pastime.

ADVERB Adverbs are normally used with a verb to add extra information by indicating how the action is done (adverbs of manner), *when*, *where* and with *how much intensity* the action is done (adverbs of time, place and intensity), or *to what extent* the action is done (adverbs of quantity). Adverbs may also be used with an adjective or another adverb, eg a *very* attractive girl, *very* well.

AGREEMENT In Italian, words such as adjectives, articles and pronouns are said to agree in number and gender with the word they refer to. This means that their ending (or form) changes according to the *number* of the noun (singular or plural) and its *gender* (masculine or feminine).

ANTECEDENT The antecedent of a relative pronoun is the word or words to which the relative pronoun refers. The antecedent is usually found directly before the relative pronoun, eg in the sentence I know *the man* who did this, the man is the antecedent of who.

APPOSITION A word or a phrase is said to be in apposition to another when it is placed directly after it without any joining word, eg Mr Jones, *our bank manager*, rang today.

ARTICLE *See* DEFINITE ARTICLE, INDEFINITE ARTICLE *and* PARTITIVE ARTICLE.

AUGMENTATIVE An augmentative is added to a noun to indicate largeness, eg ragazzo ('boy'), ragazzone ('big boy').

AUXILIARY Auxiliary verbs are used to form compound tenses of other verbs, eg *have* in I *have* seen or *will* in she *will* go. The main auxiliary verbs in Italian are avere ('to have') and essere ('to be'). *See* MODAL AUXILIARIES.

CARDINAL Cardinal numbers are numbers such as one, two, ten, fourteen, as opposed to *ordinal* numbers (eg first, second).

CLAUSE A clause is a group of words which contains at least a subject and a verb: he said is a clause. A clause often contains more than this basic information, eg *he said* this to her yesterday. Sentences can be made up of several clauses, eg he said / he'd call me / if he were free. *See* SENTENCE.

COMPARATIVE The comparative forms of adjectives and adverbs allow us to compare two things, persons or actions. In English, more ... than, ...er than, less ... than and as ... as are used for comparison.

COMPOUND TENSES Compound tenses are tenses consisting of more than one element. In Italian, the compound tenses of a verb are formed by the *auxiliary* verb and the *past participle*: ho visto, è venuto.

COMPOUND NOUNS   Compound nouns are nouns made up of two or more separate words. English examples are **goalkeeper** or **dinner party**.

CONDITIONAL   This mood is used to describe what someone would do, or something that would happen if a condition was fulfilled, eg I *would come* if I was well, the chair *would have broken* if he had sat on it. It also indicates the future in the past, eg he said he *would come*.

CONJUGATION   The conjugation of a verb is the set of different forms taken in the particular tenses of that verb.

CONJUNCTION   Conjunctions are used to link different clauses. They may be coordinating or subordinating. Coordinating conjunctions are words like **and, but, or**, subordinating conjunctions are words like **because, after, although**.

COUNTABLE   A noun is countable if it can form a plural and if it can be used with the indefinite article. Examples of countable nouns are **house, car, sweater**.

DEFINITE ARTICLE   The definite article is **the** in English and **il, lo, la, l', i, gli** and **le** in Italian.

DEMONSTRATIVE   Demonstrative adjectives such as **this, that, these** and pronouns such as **this one, that one** are used to point out a particular person or object.

DIMINUTIVE   A diminutive is added to a noun or an adjective to indicate smallness or a favourable attitude by the speaker, eg **ragazzo** ('boy'), **ragazzino** ('small boy').

DIRECT OBJECT   A direct object is a noun or a pronoun which in English follows a verb without any linking preposition, eg I met *a friend*. Note that in English a preposition is often omitted, eg in **I sent him a present, him** is equivalent to **to him** and **a present** is the direct object.

ELISION Elision consists in replacing the last letter of certain words (lo, la, una, di) with an apostrophe (') before a word starting with a *vowel* or a *silent h*, eg l'uomo, un'amica, d'arancia, d'hotel.

ENDING The ending of a verb is determined by the *person* (1st/2nd/3rd) and *number* (singular/plural) of its subject. In Italian, most tenses have six different endings. The ending of a noun can often indicate whether it is masculine or feminine and singular or plural. *See* PERSON *and* NUMBER.

EXCLAMATION An exclamation is a word or sentence used to express surprise, annoyance *etc*, eg what!, wow!, how lucky!, what a nice day!

FEMININE *See* GENDER.

GENDER The gender of a noun indicates whether the noun is *masculine* or *feminine*. In Italian, the gender of a noun is not always determined by the sex of what it refers to.

GERUND A gerund (also called a 'verbal noun' in English) is like the word skiing in *skiing is fun* and waiting in I'm fed up with *waiting*. In Italian, gerunds cannot be nouns.

IDIOMATIC EXPRESSIONS Idiomatic expressions (or idioms) are expressions which cannot normally be translated word for word. For example, it's raining cats and dogs is translated by piove a catinelle (literally: 'it's raining by the basinful').

IMPERATIVE This mood is used for giving orders, eg stop!, don't go! or for making suggestions, eg let's go.

INDEFINITE Indefinite pronouns and adjectives are words that do not refer to a definite person or object, eg each, someone, every.

INDEFINITE ARTICLE The indefinite article is a, an in English and un, uno, una, un' in Italian.

INDICATIVE The indicative is the form of a verb normally used in making statements or asking questions, eg **I like, he came, we are trying, do you see?** It is opposed to the subjunctive, conditional and imperative.

INDIRECT OBJECT An indirect object is a pronoun or noun which follows a verb indirectly, sometimes with a linking preposition (usually to), eg **I spoke to *my friend/him*, she gave *him* a kiss.**

INFINITIVE The infinitive is the basic form of the verb as found in dictionaries. Thus **to eat, to finish, to take** are infinitives. In Italian, the infinitive is recognizable by its ending: -are, -ere or -ire (eg amare, vedere, finire).

INTERROGATIVE Interrogative words are used to ask a ***question***. This may be a direct question (***when*** will you arrive?) or an indirect question (**I don't know *when*** he'll arrive). *See* QUESTION.

MASCULINE *See* GENDER.

MODAL AUXILIARIES In Italian, the modal auxiliaries are dovere ('to have to'), potere ('to be able to') and volere ('to want to').

MOOD This is the name given to the four main areas within which a verb is conjugated. *See* INDICATIVE, SUBJUNCTIVE, CONDITIONAL, IMPERATIVE.

NOUN A noun is a word or a group of words which refers to a living creature, a thing, a place or an abstract idea, eg **postman, cat, shop, passport, life.**

NUMBER The number of a noun indicates whether the noun is ***singular*** or ***plural***. A singular noun refers to one single thing or person, eg **boy, train** and a plural noun to more than one, eg **boys, trains.**

OBJECT *See* DIRECT OBJECT, INDIRECT OBJECT.

ORDINAL   Ordinal numbers are first, second, third, fourth *etc.*

PARTITIVE ARTICLE   The partitive articles are some and any in English and del, dello, della, dell', dei, degli and delle, (as in del pane, delle banane *etc*) in Italian.

PASSATO REMOTO   This term has been used in the conjugation tables for the simple past tense known in English as the *past definite* or *past historic*, eg I ate.

PASSIVE   A verb is used in the passive when the subject of the verb does not perform the action but is subjected to it. The passive is often formed with a part of the verb to be and the past participle of the verb, eg he was rewarded.

PAST PARTICIPLE   The past participle of a verb is the form which is used after to have in English, eg ha mangiato della pasta (he/she has *eaten* some pasta), Simona è partita per Napoli (Simona has *left* for Naples).

PERSON   In any tense, there are three persons in the singular (1st: I ..., 2nd: you ..., 3rd: he/she ...), and three in the plural (1st: we ..., 2nd: you ..., 3rd: they ...). *See also* ENDING.

PERSONAL PRONOUNS   Personal pronouns stand for a noun. They usually accompany a verb and can be either the subject (I, you, he/she/it, we, they) or the object of the verb (me, you, him/her/it, us, them). Personal pronouns are also commonly used with prepositions (eg with *me*, for *you*).

PLURAL   *See* NUMBER.

POSSESSIVE   Possessive adjectives and pronouns are used to indicate possession or ownership. They are words like my/mine, your/yours, our/ours.

PREPOSITION   Prepositions are words such as with, in, to, at. They are followed by a noun or a pronoun.

PRESENT PARTICIPLE The present participle is the verb form which ends in **-ing** in English and **-ente/-ante** in Italian.

PRONOUN This is a word which stands for a noun. The main categories of pronouns are:

- ❏ *Relative pronouns* (eg who, which, that)
- ❏ *Interrogative pronouns* (eg who?, what?, which?)
- ❏ *Demonstrative pronouns* (eg this, that, these)
- ❏ *Possessive pronouns* (eg mine, yours, his)
- ❏ *Personal pronouns* (eg you, him, us)
- ❏ *Reflexive pronouns* (eg myself, himself)
- ❏ *Indefinite pronouns* (eg something, all)

QUESTION There are two question forms: **direct** questions stand on their own and require a question mark at the end, eg **when will he come?**; indirect questions are introduced by a clause and require no question mark, eg *I wonder* when he will come.

REFLEXIVE Reflexive verbs 'reflect' the action back onto the subject, eg I dressed myself. They are always found with a reflexive pronoun and are much more common in Italian than in English.

SENTENCE A sentence is a group of words made up of one or more clauses (*see* CLAUSE) and forming a complete grammatical structure. The end of a sentence is indicated by a punctuation mark (usually a full stop, a question mark or an exclamation mark).

SIMPLE TENSE Simple tenses are tenses in which the verb consists of one word only, eg abito, partirà.

SINGULAR *See* NUMBER.

STEM *See* VERB STEM.

SUBJECT The subject of a verb is the noun or pronoun which performs the action. In the sentences *the train* left early and *she bought* a CD, the train and she are the subjects.

SUBJUNCTIVE The subjunctive is a verb form which is rarely used in English, eg if I *were* you, God *save* the Queen, but is common in Italian.

SUPERLATIVE The form of an adjective or an adverb which, in English, is marked by the most ..., the ...est or the least ....

TENSE Verbs are used in tenses, which tell us when an action takes place, eg in the present, the past, the future.

VERB A verb is a word which usually describes an action, eg to sing, to work, to watch or the existence of a state, eg to be, to have, to hope.

VERB STEM The stem of a verb is its basic unit to which the various endings are added. To find the stem of an Italian verb remove -are, -ere or -ire from the infinitive.

VOICE The two voices of a verb are its *active* and *passive* forms.

1 ARTICLES

A THE DEFINITE ARTICLE

1 Forms

In English, there is only one form of the definite article: **the**. In Italian there are six forms, depending on the gender, the number and the initial letter of the noun following the article:

	SINGULAR	PLURAL
masculine	il	i
	lo (l')	gli
feminine	la (l')	le

Masculine

a) il/i are used:

    i) before nouns beginning with a consonant:

      il libro/i libri   **il disco/i dischi**
      the book/the books   the record/the records

    ii) before nouns beginning with j (pronounced as in 'jeans'):

      il juke-box/i juke-box
      the juke-box/the juke-boxes

b) lo/gli are used:

    i) before nouns beginning with s + consonant (sp-, st-, *etc*):

      lo studente/gli studenti   **lo squalo/ gli squali**
      the student/the students   the shark/the sharks

      lo scultore/gli scultori   **lo sciatore/gli sciatori**
      the sculptor/the sculptors   the skier/the skiers

ii) before z and x:

lo zio/gli zii
the uncle/the uncles

lo xilofono/gli xilofoni
the xylophone/the xylophones

iii) before ps, gn:

lo psicologo/gli psicologi
the psychologist/the psychologists

lo gnomo/gli gnomi
the gnome/the gnomes

iv) before i, j and y (all pronounced i) + vowel:

lo yoghurt/gli yoghurt
the yoghurt/the yoghurts

lo ione/gli ioni
the ion/the ions

c) l'/gli are used before words beginning with a vowel:

l'albergo/gli alberghi
the hotel/the hotels

Feminine

a) la/le are used with words beginning with a consonant:

la penna/le penne
the pen/the pens

b) l'/le are used with words beginning with a vowel:

l'autostrada/le autostrade
the motorway/the motorways

l'entrata/le entrate
the entrance/the entrances

Note

If the noun is preceded by an adjective, the article is placed before the adjective and agrees with it:

il bravo studente
the good student

Note also that if it precedes a foreign word, the article is chosen according to the initial sound in Italian, regardless of spelling:

lo champagne
the champagne

lo shampoo
the shampoo

il walzer
the waltz

2 Use

As in English, the definite article is used when referring to something known or given:

gli amici di cui ti ho parlato
the friends I told you about

la ragazza di Stefano
Stefano's girlfriend

However, the definite article is used far more frequently in Italian than in English, in particular in the following cases:

a) *With uncountable nouns*

l'uguaglianza tra gli uomini è un sogno
equality among men is a dream

l'oro e l'argento sono metalli preziosi
gold and silver are precious metals

l'italiano non è difficile da imparare
Italian is not difficult to learn

il verde è il colore della speranza
green is the colour of hope

il caffè è la bevanda preferita degli Italiani
coffee is the Italians' favourite drink

b) *With nouns indicating categories or species, both singular and plural*

il cane è il miglior amico dell'uomo
a dog is man's best friend

i cani e i gatti sono animali domestici
dogs and cats are domestic animals

c) *With possessives*

il tuo vestito è nella mia camera
your dress is in my bedroom

> ### Note
>
> The article is not used with the *singular* names of relatives preceded by the possessive adjectives mio, tuo, suo, nostro and vostro (ie all but loro):
>
> | | |
> |---|---|
> | **mio padre** | **tua madre** |
> | my father | your mother |
> | **il loro padre** | **le mie sorelle** |
> | their father | my sisters |

The article is used in familiar expressions and with diminutives:

la mia mamma	**la nostra sorellina**
my mum	our little sister

See also pp 92-6.

d) *With geographical nouns except for towns and several islands*

l'Italia ha la forma di uno stivale
Italy is the shape of a boot

l'Arno passa per Firenze
the Arno flows through Florence

Venezia è una città romantica
Venice is a romantic city

Capri e Ischia sono due piccole isole
Capri and Ischia are two small islands

But:

  i) articles are used when towns and some islands are accompanied by an adjective or by a complement:

la bella Capri	**la Venezia dei Dogi**
beautiful Capri	the Venice of the Doges

ii) when a country, region or continent is preceded by 'in', it does not take the article, provided that it is not plural or accompanied by an adjective or a complement:

vado in Sicilia
I'm going to Sicily

mi piacerebbe vivere in Francia
I'd like to live in France

iii) Andorra, Gibilterra (Gibraltar), Monaco, Panama, Israele and San Marino never take the article:

San Marino è la repubblica più piccola del mondo
San Marino is the smallest republic in the world

e) *With certain expressions of time*

il 1968 fu un anno difficile
1968 was a difficult year

sono le tre
it's three o'clock

f) *With certain expressions of quantity*

il due per cento
two per cent

40 km all'ora *(all' = a preposition + l' article)*
40 km per hour

10 euro all'ora *(all' = a preposition + l' article)*
10 euros an hour

3 euro al chilo *(al = a preposition + il article)*
3 euros a kilo

g) *With titles*

il signor Rossi
Mr Rossi

il dottor Franchi
Dr Franchi

Note that the article is not used in direct speech:

'Buon giorno, professor Bianchi'
'Good morning, Professor Bianchi'

B THE INDEFINITE ARTICLE

1 Forms

The forms of the indefinite article are the same as those of the numeral uno (one):

vuoi un libro?
do you want a book?
do you want one book?

masculine	un
	uno
feminine	una
	un'

Masculine

a) un is used before words beginning with a consonant or a vowel:

un libro   **un albergo**
a book   a hotel

b) uno is used before words beginning with s + consonant, before z, x, gn and ps, and before i, j and y (all pronounced i) + vowel:

uno studente   **uno ione**
a student   an ion
uno gnomo   **uno psicologo**
a gnome   a psychologist
uno zio   **uno yoghurt**
an uncle   a yoghurt

Feminine

a) una is used before words beginning with a consonant and with i + another vowel:

una strada   **una iena**
a road   a hyena

b) un' is used before vowels:

un'autostrada   **un'amica**
a motorway   a friend *(fem)*

But: **un amico**
        a friend *(masc)*

> ## Note
>
> If the noun is *preceded* by an adjective, the article is placed
> *before* the adjective and agrees with it:
>
> **un bravo studente**   **una cara amica**
> a good student   a close friend
>
> Note also that if the article precedes foreign words, it is chosen
> according to the initial sound in Italian, regardless of spelling:
>
> **uno shampoo**   **un walzer**
> a shampoo   a waltz

Plural

un/uno/una/un' have no plural form, although they could be
replaced by the partitive articles (*see* pp 22-4) or by the adjectives
qualche or alcuni/e (*see* pp 97-102).

2 Use

On the whole, the indefinite article is used in the same way as its
English equivalent:

uno studente   **una scala**
a student   a ladder

However, the indefinite article is used far more frequently in Italian
than in English, in particular in the following cases:

a) *With uncountable nouns*

ci vuole una grande pazienza per fare questo lavoro
great patience is required to do this job

questo è un alluminio molto resistente
this is very strong aluminium

ha una bellezza straordinaria
she has extraordinary beauty

b) *With approximate numbers* (*see also* chapter 10, p 242)

una decina   **un centinaio**
about ten   about a hundred

c) *To convey a sense of indeterminacy*
ho camminato per un tre chilometri
I walked for about three kilometres

> *But:* **che ragazza graziosa!**   **un chilo e mezzo**
> what a nice girl!   a kilo and a half

C THE PARTITIVE ARTICLE

The Italian partitive article corresponds to 'some'/'any' in English.

1 Forms

The partitive article is formed by combining the preposition di with
the definite article:

MASCULINE	FEMININE
SINGULAR	
di + il = del	di + la = della
di + lo = dello	di + l' = dell'
di + l' = dell'	
PLURAL	
di + i = dei	di + le = delle
di + gli = degli	

Note that like definite articles, partitive articles are chosen
according to the gender, the number and the initial letter of the
noun which follows (*see* pp 15–16):

del vino	**dello zucchero**	**dell'olio**
some wine	some sugar	some oil

della carta	**dell'acqua**	
some paper	some water	
dei libri	**degli errori**	**delle lettere**
some books	some mistakes	some letters

2 Use

a) *Singular*

This is only used with uncountable nouns both in affirmative and interrogative sentences:

ho comprato del pane	**incontrai della gente**
I've bought some bread	I met some people
volete del burro?	**avete della farina?**
do you want some butter?	do you have any flour?

b) *Plural*

This is used both in affirmative and interrogative sentences:

vorrei delle arance	**comprammo degli spinaci**
I'd like some oranges	we bought some spinach
ha lasciato delle impronte	
he/she left some fingerprints	
hai incontrato dei ragazzi simpatici?	
did you meet some nice boys?	

3 Omission

a) In Italian it is possible to omit the partitive article more often than in English, especially when the idea of quantity is not important to the speaker:

c'era polvere dappertutto	**avete latte scremato?**
there was dust everywhere	do you have any skimmed milk?
avete giacche di pelle?	**abbiamo mangiato patatine fritte**
do you have any leather jackets?	we ate chips
affittano appartamenti per l'estate	
they rent out flats for the summer	

b) In particular, the partitive article is omitted:

  i) *always* in negative sentences:

non ho amici	**non c'è pane**
I've got no friends	there isn't any bread

  ii) *always* after the preposition di:

a casa di amici	**ho voglia di fragole**
at friends'	I would like (some) strawberries

  iii) *preferably* after other prepositions:

rispose con parole gentili	**una torta con fragole**
he/she replied with kind words	a cake with strawberries

4 Alternatives

a) qualche (some/any) is used only with singular, countable nouns although there is a plural sense:

ho letto qualche racconto di Calvino
I read some short stories by Calvino

b) un po' di (a little/some/any) can be used as an alternative to both singular and sometimes plural partitive articles:

vuoi un po' di latte?	**vorrei un po' di fragole**
do you want some milk?	I'd like some strawberries

c) alcuni/e (some/a few) can be used as an alternative to the plural partitive article:

ho fatto alcuni esercizi di grammatica
I did some grammar exercises

d) nessun(o)/nessuna or alcun(o)/alcuna (no/not any) can be used before countable nouns but only in the singular:

non ho letto nessun libro di Moravia
non ho letto alcun libro di Moravia
I haven't read any book(s) by Moravia

qui non c'è nessuna penna che funzioni
qui non c'è alcuna penna che funzioni
there's no pen here that works

2 NOUNS

A noun is a word or group of words which refers to a person, an animal, a thing, a place or an abstract idea.

A GENDER

All Italian nouns are masculine or feminine; there is no neuter as in English. Although no absolute rule can be stated, the gender can often be determined either by the *meaning* or the *ending* of the noun.

1 By meaning

Masculine

a) *Names of male people and animals*

l'uomo	**il padre**	**il cane**
the man	the father	the dog
il ragazzo	**il leone**	**il gatto**
the boy	the lion	the cat

Note, however, that there are some nouns denoting people which, although feminine in gender, refer to a man or could be used when referring to both a woman and a man:

la guardia	**la spia**	**la guida**
the guard	the spy	the guide
la vittima	**la persona**	
the victim	the person	

Note too that there are some nouns denoting animals which, although feminine in gender, refer both to male and female animals (*see also* p 27):

la giraffa	**la pantera**	**la tigre**
the giraffe	the panther	the tiger

b) *Languages*

l'italiano	**il francese**	**lo spagnolo**
Italian	French	Spanish

c) *Names of common trees and shrubs*

	il melo	**il pino**	**il biancospino**
	the apple tree	the pine tree	the hawthorn
	il pioppo	**il noce**	**il castagno**
	the poplar	the walnut tree	the chestnut tree
But:	**la betulla**	**la palma**	**la quercia**
	the birch	the palm tree	the oak

d) *Names of mountains, rivers, lakes, seas, oceans*

	gli Appennini	**il Monte Bianco**	**l'Arno**
	the Apennines	Mont Blanc	the Arno
	il Garda	**l'Adriatico**	**il Pacifico**
	Lake Garda	the Adriatic	the Pacific
But:	**le Alpi**	**le Dolomiti**	**la Senna**
	the Alps	the Dolomites	the Seine

e) *Points of the compass*

il nord	**il sud**	**l'est**	**l'ovest**
the north	the south	the east	the west
il meridione	**il ponente**		
the South	the West		

f) *Names of months and days*

	gennaio	**marzo**	**il lunedì**	**il sabato**
	January	March	Monday	Saturday
But:	**la domenica**			
	Sunday			

g) *Metals and chemical elements*

l'oro	**il ferro**	**l'ottone**
gold	iron	brass
il carbone	**l'ossigeno**	**l'uranio**
coal	oxygen	uranium

h) *Colours*

il bianco	**il rosso**	**il verde**
white	red	green

Feminine

a) *Names of female people and animals*

la donna	**la madre**	**la gatta**
the woman	the mother	the cat

Note, however, that there are some nouns denoting people which, although masculine in gender, generally refer to women, although they could also refer to men (*see* p 29):

il soprano	**il contralto**
the soprano	the contralto

Note too that there are some nouns denoting animals which, although masculine in gender, can refer both to male and female animals (*see also* p 25):

il leopardo	**il corvo**	**lo scimpanzè**
the leopard	the raven	the chimpanzee

b) *Names of fruit and nuts*

	la mela	**la pera**	**l'uva**
	the apple	the pear	the grapes
	la ciliegia	**l'arancia**	**la noce**
	the cherry	the orange	the walnut
But:	**il limone**	**il melone**	**il pompelmo**
	the lemon	the melon	the grapefruit

c) *Continents*

l'Europa	**l'America**	**l'Australia**
Europe	America	Australia

27

d) *Countries*

	l'Italia	**la Francia**	**la Gran Bretagna**
	Italy	France	Great Britain
	l'Argentina	**la Germania**	**la Danimarca**
	Argentina	Germany	Denmark
But:	**il Belgio**	**il Canada**	**l'Egitto**
	Belgium	Canada	Egypt
	il Giappone	**il Portogallo**	**gli Stati Uniti**
	Japan	Portugal	the United States

e) *Names of islands*

	la Sicilia	**la Sardegna**	**l'Elba**	**le Canarie**
	Sicily	Sardinia	Elba	the Canaries
But:	**il Madagascar**		**il Borneo**	
	Madagascar		Borneo	

f) *Cities and towns*

	Torino	**Milano**	**Venezia**	**Mosca**
	Turin	Milan	Venice	Moscow
But:	**il Cairo**			
	Cairo			

g) *Many abstract nouns*

	la bontà	**la libertà**	**la virtù**
	goodness	freedom	virtue
	la chimica	**la pace**	**la giustizia**
	chemistry	peace	justice
But:	**l'amore** *(masc)*	**l'egoismo** *(masc)*	**il coraggio**
	love	egoism	courage

2 By ending

a) Almost all nouns ending in -o are masculine:

	il quadro	il prezzo	il libro
	the picture	the price	the book
But:	**la mano**	**la radio**	**la dinamo**
	the hand	the radio	the dynamo
	la foto	**la moto**	
	the photo	the motorbike	

Note, however, that eco (echo) is both masculine and feminine in the singular, but it is always masculine in the plural (gli echi).

b) Most nouns ending in -a are feminine:

la casa	la sedia	la pianta
the house	the chair	the plant

Note, however, that there are several masculine nouns ending in -a (mostly derived from Greek):

il profeta	il dramma	il problema
the prophet	the drama	the problem
il tema	il poeta	il papa
the theme	the poet	the pope

Note also that there are some nouns ending in -cida and -ista which can be either gender:

il giornalista	la giornalista
the journalist *(male)*	the journalist *(female)*
un artista	un'artista
an artist *(male)*	an artist *(female)*
un omicida	un'omicida
a murderer	a murderess

c) Nouns ending in -e can be either masculine or feminine:

la notte	la ragione	la mente
the night	the reason	the mind
il fiume	il dente	il ponte
the river	the tooth	the bridge

i) However, most nouns ending in -zione, -sione, -gione, -udine, -ite, -igine and those in -ice referring to women are feminine:

la soluzione the solution	**la conclusione** the conclusion
la regione the region	**l'abitudine** the habit
l'appendicite the appendicitis	**l'origine** the origin
la scrittrice the writer	

ii) Most nouns ending in -ore, -ere, -ame, -ale, -ile are masculine:

il motore the engine	**il carcere** the prison
il bestiame the cattle	**il temporale** the storm
il canile the kennel	

Note that nouns ending in -e which indicate titles (signore, professore, ingegnere, ragioniere *etc*) drop their final -e before names and surnames:

il signor Rossi Mr Rossi	**il professor Bianchi** Professor Bianchi

d) Most nouns ending in -i are feminine:

la crisi the crisis	**la tesi** the thesis	**l'analisi** the analysis

But: **il brindisi**
the toast

e) Nouns ending in -u can be either feminine or masculine:

la virtù virtue	**il bambù** bamboo

f) Nouns ending with a consonant (normally foreign words) are masculine:

	lo sport	il film	il tram
	sport	the film	the tram
But:	la hall	la star	
	the hall	the star	

B THE FORMATION OF FEMININES

1 The feminine equivalent of most masculine nouns ending in -o and -e is formed by replacing these endings with -a:

il bambino	la bambina	little boy/girl
il cavallo	la cavalla	horse/mare
l'infermiere	l'infermiera	male/female nurse
il cameriere	la cameriera	waiter/waitress

2 The feminine equivalent of some masculine nouns ending in -o, -e and -a is formed by adding -essa to their stem:

il campione	la campionessa	male/female champion
il leone	la leonessa	lion/lioness
il poeta	la poetessa	poet/poetess
il professore	la professoressa	male/female professor

3 With masculine nouns ending in -tore, the ending changes to -trice to form the feminine equivalent:

	il pittore	la pittrice	male/female painter
	il vincitore	la vincitrice	male/female winner
	l'imperatore	l'imperatrice	emperor/empress
	l'attore	l'attrice	actor/actress
	lo scrittore	la scrittrice	male/female writer
But:	il dottore	la dottoressa	male/female doctor

4 Some nouns have a common gender, that is to say they have the same endings for the masculine and feminine. They can be distinguished by the article or by the adjective which accompanies them. *See also* p 29:

a) Some nouns ending in -e:

il cantante	la cantante	male/female singer
il nipote	la nipote	nephew/niece
un agente	un'agente	male/female agent
un amante	un'amante	male/female lover

Note that these nouns have the same endings in the masculine and feminine plurals (*see* p 38):

i cantanti	le cantanti	male/female singers

b) All nouns ending in -ista and -cida:

il pianista	la pianista	male/female pianist
un artista	un'artista	male/female artist
il suicida	la suicida	male/female suicide
un omicida	un'omicida	murderer/murderess

Note that these nouns have different endings for the masculine and feminine plurals (*see* p 37):

i pianisti	le pianiste	male/female pianists

c) Some nouns derived from Greek, ending in -a:

il collega	la collega	male/female colleague
un atleta	un'atleta	male/female athlete
il pediatra	la pediatra	male/female paediatrician

Note that these nouns have different endings for the masculine and feminine plurals (*see* p 37):

gli atleti	le atlete	male/female athletes

Note that the gender of articles and adjectives should agree with the gender of these nouns:

un cantante famoso	**una cantante famosa**
a famous singer *(male)*	a famous singer *(female)*
un bravo giornalista	**una brava giornalista**
a good journalist *(male)*	a good journalist *(female)*

5 Some nouns indicating professions or positions are used in the masculine to refer to women as well, since their regular feminine form would give the noun an ironic or a pejorative significance:

il medico	doctor
l'avvocato	lawyer
il ministro	minister

6 Some names of animals are only masculine or only feminine and their feminine and masculine equivalents can be formed either by adding the words femmina/maschio or by placing the expressions la femmina del/il maschio della in front of the noun in question:

il leopardo	il leopardo femmina/la femmina del leopardo
the leopard	the female leopard
la giraffa	la giraffa maschio/il maschio della giraffa
the giraffe	the male giraffe

7 The following feminine nouns are irregular:

il dio	la dea	god/goddess
lo stregone	la strega	wizard/witch
l'eroe	l'eroina	hero/heroine
il re	la regina	king/queen
lo zar	la zarina	tsar/tsarina
il gallo	la gallina	cock/hen

8 The feminine form of masculine nouns for names of trees refers to the fruit of the respective tree:

il melo	la mela	apple tree/apple
il pero	la pera	pear tree/pear

9 Some nouns have only one gender – either masculine or feminine – which could refer to both sexes:

una persona	a person *(male/female)*	**la sentinella**	the sentry *(male/female)*
la spia	the spy *(male/female)*	**il ministro**	the minister *(male/female)*
un medico	a doctor *(male/female)*	**il soprano**	the soprano *(male/female)*

mio padre è una persona straordinaria
my father is an extraordinary person

Maria è un bravo medico   **la tigre addomesticata**
Maria is a good doctor   the tame tiger

10 Some nouns change their meaning according to gender, but their endings do not change:

il fine	aim	**la fine**	end
il capitale	capital *(money)*	**la capitale**	capital *(city)*
il radio	radium	**la radio**	radio
il fronte	front	**la fronte**	forehead

C THE FORMATION OF PLURALS

1 Nouns ending in -o

a) Masculine nouns ending in -o change to -i:

il libro	**i libri**	book
il sasso	**i sassi**	stone
il tavolo	**i tavoli**	table
il gatto	**i gatti**	cat

Note that some nouns ending in -o, although changing to -i for the plural, also change their stem:

il dio	**gli dei**	god
il tempio	**i templi**	temple
l'uomo	**gli uomini**	man

b) Feminine nouns ending in -o remain unchanged in the plural (*see also* p 40):

	la moto	le moto	motorbike
	la foto	le foto	photo
But:	la mano	le mani	hand

c) Nouns ending in -io with an unstressed -i- change to -i:

l'esempio	gli esempi	example
l'occhio	gil occhi	eye
il figlio	i figli	son

Note that some nouns ending in -io can be confused in the plural with nouns which have a different meaning but the same spelling. In these cases an accent or a double i can be used to differentiate them:

il principe	i principi	prince
	i prìncipi	
il principio	i principi	principle
	i princìpi	
	i principî	
	i principii	

d) Nouns ending in -io with a stressed -i- change to -ii:

lo zio	gli zii	uncle
il pendio	i pendii	slope
il mormorio	i mormorii	murmur

e) Nouns ending in -co and -go change to -chi, -ci, -ghi and -gi in the plural but follow no absolute rule. However, there are two main categories:

  i) if the stress falls on the penultimate syllable, the ending changes to -chi and -ghi, although there are various exceptions:

	il cuoco	i cuochi	cook
	il fuoco	i fuochi	fire
	l'albergo	gli alberghi	hotel

	il fungo	i funghi	mushroom
But:	l'amico	gli amici	friend
	il porco	i porci	pig

ii) if the stress falls before the penultimate syllable, the ending changes to -ci and -gi, although there are various exceptions:

	il medico	i medici	doctor
	il portico	i portici	porch
	il teologo	i teologi	theologian
	l'asparago	gli asparagi	asparagus
But:	il carico	i carichi	load
	l'obbligo	gli obblighi	obligation

Note that some nouns have a plural both in -ci/-gi and -chi/-ghi:

il manico	i manici/i manichi	handle

Note too that nouns ending in -logo generally change to -logi if they refer to people, and -loghi if they refer to things:

lo psicologo	gli psicologi	psychologist
l'archeologo	gli archeologi	archaeologist
il dialogo	i dialoghi	dialogue
il catalogo	i cataloghi	catalogue

f) Some masculine nouns ending in -o change gender in the plural and their ending becomes -a (*see* pp 40-1):

il centinaio	le centinaia	about a hundred
l'uovo	le uova	egg

2 Nouns ending in -a

a) Feminine nouns ending in -a change to -e:

	la casa	le case	house
	la ragazza	le ragazze	girl
	la leonessa	le leonesse	lioness
But:	arma and ala are exceptions as their endings change to -i:		
	l'arma	le armi	weapon
	l'ala	le ali	wing

b) Masculine nouns ending in -a (mostly of Greek origin) change to -i:

il problema	i problemi	problem
il clima	i climi	climate
il fantasma	i fantasmi	ghost
l'atleta	gli atleti	athlete
il papa	i papi	pope
il pigiama	i pigiami	pyjamas

Note that some nouns ending in -a change to -i in the plural if they refer to men and -e if they refer to women:

i) nouns ending in -ista and -cida:

l'artista	gli artisti	artist *(male)*
l'artista	le artiste	artist *(female)*
l'omicida	gli omicidi	murderer
l'omicida	le omicide	murderess

ii) some nouns of Greek origin:

il collega	i colleghi	male colleague
la collega	le colleghe	female colleague

Note that some masculine nouns in -a do not change in the plural (*see also* p 39):

il boa	i boa	boa

c) Nouns ending in -ca and -ga change to -che and -ghe if feminine and -chi and -ghi if masculine:

la banca	le banche	bank
la piaga	le piaghe	wound, scar
il monarca	i monarchi	monarch
lo stratega	gli strateghi	strategist

d) Nouns ending in -cia and -gia change to -ce and -ge if the ending is preceded by a consonant, and to -cie and -gie if it is preceded by a vowel:

la bilancia	le bilance	scales
la pioggia	le piogge	rain
la camicia	le camicie	shirt

Note that the following two nouns have two possible plural forms:

la valigia	**le valigie**	suitcase
	le valige	
la ciliegia	**le ciliegie**	cherry
	le ciliege	

e) Nouns ending in -ia, -cia, -gia, -scia with the -i- stressed retain the -i- in the plural:

la galleria	**le gallerie**	gallery
la farmacia	**le farmacie**	chemist's
la bugia	**le bugie**	lie
la scia	**le scie**	trail

f) Nouns ending in -ea change to -ee, whether the -e- is stressed or not:

l'assemblea	**le assemblee**	assembly

3 Nouns ending in -e

a) Both masculine and feminine nouns change from -e to -i:

	il fiore	**i fiori**	flower
	la cornice	**le cornici**	frame
Note:	**il bue**	**i buoi**	ox

b) Nouns having the same ending for masculine and feminine in the singular also have the same ending in the plural:

il nipote	**i nipoti**	nephew
la nipote	**le nipoti**	niece

4 Nouns which do not change in the plural

a) Nouns ending in -i:

la crisi	**le crisi**	crisis
l'alibi	**gli alibi**	alibi

b) Nouns ending in -u:

| il menu | i menu | menu |
| la gru | le gru | crane |

c) Nouns ending in -ie:

	la serie	le serie	series
But:	la superficie	le superfici	surface
	la moglie	le mogli	wife
	l'effigie	le effigi	effigy

d) Nouns ending in an accented vowel:

la città	le città	town
l'università	le università	university
il caffè	i caffè	coffee
il lunedì	i lunedì	Monday
la virtù	le virtù	virtue
il bambù	i bambù	bamboo

e) Nouns of foreign origin ending in a consonant:

il club	i club
il film	i film
lo sport	gli sport

f) Acronyms and abbreviations:

| **due BMW** | two BMWs | **molte Fiat** | a lot of Fiats |

g) Nouns which have only one syllable:

| il re | i re | king |
| lo sci | gli sci | ski |

h) A few masculine nouns ending in -a:

il cinema	i cinema	cinema
il vaglia	i vaglia	money order
il sosia	i sosia	double

i) Feminine nouns ending in -o:

la biro	le biro	biro
l'auto	le auto	car
la foto	le foto	photo
la radio	le radio	radio
la moto	le moto	motorbike
But: la mano	le mani	hand

5 Irregularities

a) A few nouns change gender in the plural and have the ending -a:

il paio	le paia	pair
il riso	le risa	laugh
l'uovo	le uova	egg
il centinaio	le centinaia	hundred
il migliaio	le migliaia	thousand
il miglio	le miglia	mile
Also: il carcere	le carceri	prison

b) A few nouns are used only in the plural:

i) nouns indicating pairs of things:

i calzoni	trousers
le forbici	scissors
gli occhiali	spectacles

ii) nouns referring to words which have a plural sense:

i viveri	provisions
i dintorni	surroundings

iii) other nouns:

le nozze	wedding
le tenebre	darkness

c) Some nouns are used only in the singular, since, as in English, they do not have a plural:

la chimica	chemistry
il tifo	typhus
il rame	copper
il latte	milk

d) A few nouns have two plurals, each with a different meaning:

il braccio	**le braccia**	**i bracci**
arm	arms *(part of body)*	arms *(of cross etc)*
il labbro	**le labbra**	**i labbri**
lip	lips *(of mouth)*	the lips *(of wound etc)*
il muro	**le mura**	**i muri**
wall	walls *(of city)*	walls *(of house)*
l'osso	**le ossa**	**gli ossi**
bone	bones *(of skeleton)*	bones *(of meat)*

e) A few nouns have two plurals without any difference in meaning:

il ginocchio	**le ginocchia**	**i ginocchi**
knee		
il lenzuolo	**le lenzuola**	**i lenzuoli**
sheet		
il grido	**le grida**	**i gridi**
shout		

f) A few nouns have two plurals and two singulars:

l'orecchio	**l'orecchia**	**gli orecchi**	**le orecchie**
ear		ears	

6 Compound nouns

Compound nouns generally behave like ordinary nouns in the plural (ie changing the end vowel). However, in some cases both elements remain unchanged, and in other cases the first element changes. In particular:

a) Nouns made up of *noun + noun* generally change their end vowel:

il pescecane	i pescecani	shark
la madreperla	le madreperle	mother-of-pearl

> ## Note
>
> - Feminine nouns containing the word **capo** remain unchanged in the plural:
>
>   **la caposquadra – le caposquadra**
>   forewoman
>
> - Masculine nouns containing the word **capo** can have various plurals and should be checked individually in a dictionary:
>
> | | |
> |---|---|
> | il capostazione – i capistazione | il capolavoro – i capolavori |
> | station master | masterpiece |

b) Nouns made up of *adjective + noun* change the end vowel:

	il bassorilievo	i bassorilievi	bas-relief
	l'altoparlante	gli altoparlanti	loudspeaker
But:	la mezzaluna	le mezzelune	half-moon
	il purosangue	i purosangue	thoroughbred

c) Nouns made up of *noun + adjective* change the end vowel of both noun and adjective:

	la cassaforte	le casseforti	safe
	la terracotta	le terrecotte	terracotta
But:	il palcoscenico	i palcoscenici	stage

d) Nouns made up of *verb + noun*:

   i) nouns made up of *verb + singular feminine noun* do not change in the plural:

il cacciavite	i cacciavite	screwdriver
il portacenere	i portacenere	ashtray
But: **l'asciugamano**	**gli asciugamani**	towel

   ii) nouns made up of *verb + singular masculine noun* change the end vowel in the plural:

il parafango	i parafanghi	mudguard
il passaporto	i passaporti	passport

   iii) nouns made up of *verb + plural noun* remain unchanged:

l'apriscatole	gli apriscatole	tin-opener
l'attaccapanni	gli attaccapanni	hanger

e) Nouns made up of *verb + verb* do not change in the plural:

il saliscendi	i saliscendi	latch

f) Nouns made up of *adverb + verb* do not change in the plural:

il benestare	i benestare	approval

g) Nouns made up of either a *preposition* or an *adverb + noun* can have various plurals and should be checked individually in a dictionary:

il senzatetto	i senzatetto	homeless person
il benefattore	i benefattori	benefactor
il contrabbasso	i contrabbassi	(double) bass
il soprannome	i soprannomi	nickname

h) When two nouns are separated by a hyphen, only the first noun changes:

il divano-letto	i divani-letto	sofa-bed

7 Collective nouns

a) Singular nouns in Italian, but plural in English:

la gente	people
la polizia	police
il bestiame	cattle

la polizia ha arrestato il ladro
the police have arrested the thief

b) Plural nouns in Italian, but singular in English:

le notizie	news
i mobili	furniture
gli spaghetti	spaghetti
i capelli	hair

ci sono buone notizie   **questi spaghetti sono buoni**
that's good news   this spaghetti's great

8 Proper nouns

a) Ordinary family names are invariable in the plural:

ho incontrato i (signori) Bragato alla festa
I met the Bragatos at the party

b) Some historical names add -i for the plural:

i Borboni   the Bourbons

SUFFIXES

In Italian the meaning of some nouns (and also of adjectives and adverbs) can be altered through the addition of suffixes (different endings) which add different shades of meaning:

a) The suffixes -ino/a, -etto/a, -ello/a, -ellino/a are generally diminutives:

ragazzo	boy	**ragazzino**	small boy
casa	house	**casetta**	pretty little house
secchio	bucket	**secchiello**	small bucket
rosa	rose	**rosellina**	lovely little rose

b) The suffixes -one/a increase the idea of size or strengthen the meaning of the original word:

ragazzo	boy	**ragazzone**	big boy

c) The suffixes -astro/a, -accio/a, -attolo/a, -ucolo/a, -upolo/a give the noun negative connotations:

poeta	poet	**poeta**stro	bad poet
ragazzo	boy	**ragazzaccio**	bad boy
uomo	man	**omiciattolo**	worthless/small, ugly man
professore	teacher	**professorucolo**	bad teacher
casa	house	**casupola**	hovel

Note, however, that many words ending in these suffixes have separate meanings, and not every word can be altered as described above:

posta	post (office)	**postino**	postman
borsa	bag	**borsetta**	handbag
carta	paper	**cartone**	cardboard

E USE OF CAPITAL LETTERS

There are some differences in the use of capital letters between English and Italian. Capitals are not used in Italian for:

a) *Nationalities*

un italiano e un inglese
an Italian and an Englishman

> *Note*
>
> Plural nouns indicating a race can be capitalized in Italian:
>
> **gli Americani**
> Americans
>
> However, the plural adjective is never capitalized:
>
> **i soldati americani**
> American soldiers

b) *Inhabitants of towns* (both nouns and adjectives)

una fiorentina   **un londinese**
a Florentine   a Londoner

c) *Languages*

studio il francese
I'm studying French

d) *Months and days of the week*

aprile   **sabato**
April   Saturday

e) *Kings, popes, bishops etc*

la regina Elisabetta
Queen Elizabeth

f) san/santa/santo *referring to a saint*

san Marco   **sant'Anna**
Saint Mark   Saint Anne

Note that these words are capitalized when referring to the name of a church:

la basilica di San Marco
Saint Mark's basilica

3 ADJECTIVES

Adjectives are variable parts of speech which accompany a noun to describe its qualities or to define it better:

un ristorante italiano
an Italian restaurant

un celebre ballerino
a famous dancer

una spiaggia affollata
a crowded beach

un'avventura emozionante
an exciting adventure

A AGREEMENT OF ADJECTIVES

In Italian adjectives agree in gender and number with the noun they qualify. This means that, unlike English adjectives, which don't change, Italian adjectives have different forms which are determined by the noun they go with:

il vestito rosso
the red dress

i fiori rossi
the red flowers

la camicia rossa
the red shirt

le matite rosse
the red pencils

Note

- When two or more singular words share the same adjective, this adjective will be in the plural:

  una **chiesa** e una **piazza** moderne
  a modern church and square

- If one of these words is masculine, the adjective will be masculine plural:

  il **ragazzo** e la **ragazza** cinesi
  the Chinese boy and girl

> *Note—cont'd*
>
> **una gonna, una giacca e** un cappello **neri**
> a black skirt, jacket and hat
>
> - However, if the adjective precedes the series of nouns, it agrees
>   with the nearest one:
>
> **belle ville e** castelli   **bei parchi e** fontane
> beautiful villas and castles   beautiful parks and fountains

B THE FORMATION OF FEMININES

1 Adjectives ending in -o form their feminine with -a:

un bambino contento   **una bambina contenta**
a happy boy   a happy girl

2 Adjectives ending in -e do not change in the feminine:

un esercizio difficile   **una lezione difficile**
a difficult exercise   a difficult lesson

3 Adjectives ending in -tore form their feminine with -trice,
as for nouns (*see* p 31):

il gruppo vincitore   **la squadra vincitrice**
the winning group   the winning team

4 Adjectives ending in -ista and -cida have the same
endings for the masculine and the feminine (*see* p 32):

un ragazzo egoista   **una ragazza egoista**
a selfish boy   a selfish girl

5 Adjectives of foreign origin do not have a feminine form:

il concerto rock   **la musica rock**
a rock concert   rock music

C THE FORMATION OF PLURALS

1 Adjectives ending in -o and -a have plural forms in -i for the masculine and -e for the feminine:

degli uomini anziani
some old men

delle donne anziane
some old women

2 Adjectives ending in -e have plural forms in -i:

dei prati verdi
some green meadows

delle valli verdi
some green valleys

3 Adjectives with other endings:

For the formation of plurals, adjectives follow the same rules given for the plural of nouns (*see* p 34):

a) Masculine forms of adjectives ending in -io with stressed -i:

pio   **pii**   pious

b) Masculine forms of adjectives ending in -io with unstressed -i:

ampio   **ampi**   ample

c) Masculine forms of adjectives ending in -co and -go with the stress on the penultimate syllable:

	stanco	stanchi	tired
	lungo	lunghi	long
But:	amico	amici	friendly
	greco	greci	Greek

d) Masculine forms of adjectives ending in -co and -go with the stress before the penultimate syllable:

	magnifico	magnifici	magnificent
But:	carico	carichi	loaded, laden

e) Feminine forms of adjectives ending in -ca and -ga:

antica	**antiche**	ancient, antique
larga	**larghe**	wide

f) Feminine forms of adjectives in -cia and -gia preceded by a consonant:

spilorcia	**spilorce**	stingy

g) Feminine forms of adjectives in -cia and -gia preceded by a vowel:

randagia	**randagie**	stray

h) Adjectives having a common gender ending in -a for the singular, including those ending in -ista and -cida:

belga *(masc)*	**belgi**	Belgian
belga *(fem)*	**belghe**	

4 Adjectives which do not change in the plural:

a) Adjectives ending in -i:

un numero pari	**i numeri pari**
an even number	even numbers
un numero dispari	**i numeri dispari**
an odd number	odd numbers

b) Adjectives of foreign origin:

il vestito sexy	**le calze sexy**
the sexy dress	the sexy stockings
il concerto rock	**i concerti rock**
the rock concert	the rock concerts

c) Some adjectives of colour which were originally nouns in their own right:

le tende crema	**gli ombretti viola**
the cream curtains	the purple eyeshadows
le tute rosa	**le calze blu**
the pink overalls	the blue socks

Note that modified expressions of colour do not change in the plural either:

i maglioni verde acqua
the bluish-green jumpers

i rossetti rosso ciliegia
the cherry-red lipsticks

However, verde and rosso by themselves behave as regular adjectives.

 D IRREGULAR ADJECTIVES

1 bello (beautiful), when it precedes the noun it qualifies, has forms similar to those of the definite article (*see* p 15):

	SINGULAR	PLURAL
masculine	bello	begli
	bell'	
	bel	bei
feminine	bella	belle
	bell'	

un bel prato
a beautiful meadow

un bell'albero
a beautiful tree

dei begli occhi
beautiful eyes

dei bei giardini
beautiful gardens

una bella donna
a beautiful woman

delle belle ragazze
some beautiful girls

Note, however, that when it follows the noun, it retains its regular forms bello/bella/belli/belle:

un ragazzo bello
a handsome boy

una ragazza bella
a beautiful girl

i ragazzi belli
the handsome boys

le ragazze belle
the beautiful girls

Note that the demonstrative adjective quello follows the same pattern as bello (*see* pp 102-3).

2 buono (good) in the singular, when it precedes the noun it qualifies, has forms similar to those of the indefinite article (*see* pp 20-21):

un buon pranzo	**un buono stipendio**	**un buon amico**
a good lunch	a good salary	a good friend

una buona cucina	**una buon'amica/una buona amica**
good cooking	a good friend

Note the regular plural buoni, buone:

dei buoni amici	**delle buone amiche**
(some) good friends *(masc)*	(some) good friends *(fem)*

3 grande (great, big) can be shortened to gran before a noun beginning with a consonant other than z or s + consonant, gn, ps or x:

un gran pasticcio	**una gran piazza**
a great mess	a big square
una grande occasione	**un grande sciocco**
a great opportunity	a great fool

However, in most cases, gran can be replaced by grande:

un gran successo
un grande successo
a great success

Note that grande can be shortened to grand' before a noun beginning with a vowel, but grande can also be used and it is more common:

un grand'aiuto
un grande aiuto
a great help

However, it is shortened when used as an intensifier:

fa un gran caldo oggi
it is extremely hot today

4 santo (Saint):

   i) shortened to sant' before male and female names beginning
   with a vowel:

   sant'Ambrogio   **sant'Anna**
   Saint Ambrose   Saint Anne

   ii) shortened to san before male names beginning with a
   consonant other than s + consonant:

   san Pietro   **san Zaccaria**
   Saint Peter   Saint Zachariah

   iii) used in full, santo, before male names beginning with s
   followed by a consonant:

   santo Stefano
   Saint Stephen

   iv) used in full in the feminine form, santa, before female names
   beginning with a consonant:

   santa Chiara
   Saint Clare

Note, however, that frequent anomalies are found in place names:

   San Stino

 E POSITION OF ADJECTIVES

1 In Italian, adjectives usually follow the nouns they qualify:

una pizza magnifica   **un discorso interessante**
a magnificent pizza   an interesting speech

2 However, the following common adjectives usually precede the noun:

antico	ancient, antique	**giovane**	young
bello	beautiful	**grande**	great
breve	short	**largo**	wide
brutto	ugly	**lungo**	long
buono	good	**piccolo**	small
cattivo	bad	**vecchio**	old

è una bella donna
she is a beautiful woman

il brutto anatroccolo
the ugly duckling

A change in position, however, can affect the force of the adjective. The adjective is given more emphasis if it is placed after the noun:

una vecchia automobile
an old car

un'automobile vecchia
an *old* car

è una vecchia automobile
it's an old car

è un'automobile brutta e vecchia
it's an awful old car

Sometimes positioning an adjective in front of a noun can have the effect of drawing attention away from it as the main emphatic word in a description:

una proposta intelligente
an intelligent proposal

l'intelligente proposta del ministro
the minister's intelligent proposal

3 Certain adjectives should always follow the noun:

a) Adjectives indicating colour, shape, nationality and religion, and past participles used as adjectives:

la bandiera rossa
the red flag

il papa tedesco
the German pope

la tavola rotonda
the round table

la chiesa cattolica
the Catholic Church

la biancheria pulita
the clean linen

un panino mezzo mangiato
a half-eaten roll

b) Adjectives which are modified by an adverb:

una giornata abbastanza calda
a rather hot day

4 Certain adjectives change their meaning according to their position. As a general rule, when they follow the noun their meaning is literal, whereas when they precede the noun a more figurative, abstract meaning is conveyed. Certain adjectives completely change their meaning according to their position:

	BEFORE NOUN	AFTER NOUN
buono	good *(in quality)*	good *(morally)*
caro	dear *(cherished)*	dear, expensive
certo	some, certain	sure, reliable
diverso	several *(diversi)*	different
grande	great	big, tall, large
vario	several *(varii)*	different
nuovo	new *(another)*	(brand) new
povero	poor *(unfortunate)*	poor *(without money)*
semplice	just, only	simple, naive
solo	single, only	alone, lonely
unico	single	unique
vero	real	true

un buon amico a good friend	**un amico buono** a good-hearted friend
un pover' uomo a poor man *(unfortunate)*	**un uomo povero** a poor man *(without money)*
certi risultati certain results	**risultati certi** reliable results
diverse persone several people	**teorie diverse** different theories
una grande opera a great work	**una camicia grande** a large shirt

un nuovo vestito a new dress	**un'automobile nuova** a (brand) new car
un semplice ragazzo just a boy	**un ragazzo semplice** a naive boy
un vero attaccabrighe a real troublemaker	**una storia vera** a true story

5 In Italian it is possible to place one adjective before and one after the same noun:

un famoso calciatore italiano
a famous Italian footballer

 F COMPARATIVE AND SUPERLATIVE OF ADJECTIVES

Persons or things can be compared by using:

❏ the comparative form of the adjective:
more ... than, ...-er than, less ... than, as ... as

❏ the relative superlative form of the adjective:
the most ..., the ...-est, the least ...

❏ the absolute superlative form of the adjective:
very ...

1 Comparative

The comparative is formed as follows:

a) più ... (di/che) (more ... / ...-er (than))

più contento happier	**più caro** more expensive

Maria è più alta di Nadia
Maria is taller than Nadia

mio padre è più vecchio di mia madre
my father is older than my mother

b) meno ... (di/che) (less ... (than))

meno intelligente **meno reale**
less intelligent less real

Paola è meno attraente di te
Paola is less attractive than you

Note

In the above comparatives, di is usually used for 'than' before numerals, pronouns and nouns, while che is usually used for 'than' before adjectives, adverbs, prepositions, participles and infinitives:

Paola è più ricca di Giorgio
Paola is richer than Giorgio

la mia moto è costata più della tua
my motorbike cost more than yours

questo giardino è più lungo che largo
this garden is longer than it is wide

questo è un libro più divertente che istruttivo
this book is more amusing than instructive

c) (tanto) ... quanto, (così) ... come *as ... as*

il calcio è tanto popolare in Gran Bretagna quanto in Italia
football is as popular in Britain as it is in Italy

The two forms quanto and come are often interchangeable. With both, the first term is frequently omitted:

è stanca quanto me/è stanca come me
she is as tired as I am

2 Relative superlative

The relative superlative indicates that a quality is possessed in the highest degree in relation to a group of people or things.

It is formed by adding the appropriate definite article to the comparative:

il/la/i/le più ... (di)	the most ..., the ...-est (of/in)
il/la/i/le meno ... (di)	the least ... (of/in)
il più veloce	**i più intelligenti**
the fastest	the most intelligent
la più giovane della famiglia	**il corridore più veloce del mondo**
the youngest of the family	the fastest runner in the world
le persone meno attive del reparto	
the least active people in the department	

Note

- When a superlative adjective follows a noun which is preceded by the definite article, the article is not repeated:

  l'animale più fedele   **i bambini più viziati**
  the most faithful animal   the most spoilt children

- 'In' is usually translated by di:

  la ragazza più carina della scuola
  the prettiest girl in the school

  Cortina è la località più celebre delle Dolomiti
  Cortina is the most famous resort in the Dolomites

- When a possessive adjective is used, the definite article precedes the possessive and is not repeated before più:

  il suo bisogno più immediato
  his/her most immediate need

3 Absolute superlative

The absolute superlative indicates that a quality is possessed in a very high degree with no relation to other people or things. It is formed:

a) By adding -issimo/a/i/e to the adjective after dropping the final vowel:

vecchio	old	vecchissimo	very old
utile	useful	utilissimo	very useful
bella	beautiful	bellissima	very beautiful
veloci	fast	velocissimi	very fast
piccole	small	piccolissime	very small

un carissimo amico
a very dear friend

una grammatica utilissima
a very useful grammar

> ## Note
>
> • Adjectives ending in -co and -go and forming their plural with -chi and -ghi drop their final vowel and add an h before -issimo/a/i/e:
>
> antico   **un vaso antichissimo**
>   a very ancient vase
>
> • Adjectives ending in -co and -go and forming their plural with -ci and -gi simply drop their final vowel before -issimo/a/i/e:
>
> pratico   **una borsa praticissima**
>   a very handy bag
>
> • Adjectives ending in -io which drop the final -i in the plural drop both final vowels before -issimo/a/i/e:
>
> vecchio   **degli stivali vecchissimi**
>   some very old boots
>
> Note, however, that not all adjectives can have this form.

b) By placing molto or assai before the adjective:

assai bella   **molto ubriaco**
very beautiful   very drunk

c) Alternative forms:

   i) by using another adjective to strengthen the meaning of the
      first adjective:

      sono stanca morta
      I'm dead tired

   ii) by placing arci-, stra-, ultra- before the adjective:

      è straricco
      he's very rich

   iii) by repeating the adjective:

      se ne stava seduto buono buono in un angolo
      he was sitting very quietly in a corner

4 Irregular comparatives and superlatives

Some Italian adjectives have irregular as well as regular forms:

ADJECTIVE	COMPARATIVE	RELATIVE SUPERLATIVE	ABSOLUTE SUPERLATIVE
buono	migliore	il migliore	ottimo
good	better	the best	excellent
cattivo	peggiore	il peggiore	pessimo
bad	worse	the worst	very bad
grande	maggiore	il maggiore	massimo
great	greater, elder	the greatest, the eldest	very great
piccolo	minore	il minore	minimo
small	smaller, younger, lesser	the smallest, the youngest, the least	very small, minute

Regular and irregular forms are usually interchangeable:

> **è il migliore caffè che abbia mai bevuto**
> **è il più buon caffè che abbia mai bevuto**
> it's the best coffee I've ever had

Note that the forms maggiore, minore are normally used for age. In other contexts they usually mean 'greater/lesser in importance', while più grande, più piccolo mean 'greater/lesser in size':

> **la tua sorella maggiore**   **il male minore**
> your elder sister   the lesser evil
>
> **l'appartamento più piccolo**
> the smaller flat

 G SUFFIXES

As with nouns, the meaning of some adjectives can be altered through the addition of suffixes:

a) The suffixes -ino/a, etto/a, -ello/a, -ellino/a are generally diminutives:

cattivo	bad, naughty	**cattivello**	rather bad, naughty
piccola	small	**piccolina**	rather small

b) The suffixes -one/a increase the idea of size expressed by the adjective or strengthen its meaning:

simpatico	nice	**simpaticone**	rather/very nice

c) The suffixes -astro/a and -accio/a give the adjective a pejorative connotation:

ricco	rich	**riccastro**	stinking rich
rosso	red	**ha degli strani capelli rossastri**	
		he/she has strange reddish hair	

4 ADVERBS

An adverb is an invariable part of speech which, when used in conjunction with a verb, an adjective or another adverb, modifies and enriches its meaning. The main categories of adverb are those of manner, time, place, quantity and intensity, affirmation, negation and doubt.

A ADVERBS OF MANNER

These answer the question 'how?' and constitute the largest category.

1 They are commonly formed by adding -mente to the adjective (the equivalent of '-ly' in English):

a) If the adjective ends in -o, -mente is added to the feminine form:

ADJECTIVE			ADVERB	
masculine	*feminine*			
vero	vera	true	veramente	really, truly
esatto	esatta	exact	esattamente	exactly
lento	lenta	slow	lentamente	slowly
affettuoso	affettuosa	affectionate	affettuosamente	affectionately

Note the following exceptions to the rules given above:

violento	violent	**violentemente**	violently
fraudolento	fraudulent	**fraudolentemente**	fraudulently
benevolo	benevolent	**benevolmente**	benevolently
malevolo	malevolent	**malevolmente**	malevolently
leggero	light	**leggermente**	lightly

b) If the adjective ends in -e, the adverb is formed by simply adding -mente:

ADJECTIVE		ADVERB	
dolce	sweet	**dolcemente**	sweetly
cortese	polite	**cortesemente**	politely
veloce	quick	**velocemente**	quickly

c) With adjectives ending in -le and -re preceded by a vowel, the final -e is dropped:

ADJECTIVE		ADVERB	
speciale	special	**special**mente	specially
gentile	nice, kind	**gentil**mente	nicely, kindly
particolare	particular	**particolar**mente	particularly
regolare	regular	**regolar**mente	regularly

Note that where -le and -re are preceded by a consonant, formation of the adverb is regular, for example:

acre	bitter	acremente	bitterly

2 Some very common adverbs are completely irregular:

ADJECTIVE		ADVERB	
buono	good	bene	well
cattivo	bad	male	badly
migliore	better	meglio	better

3 Some adverbs have no relation to adjectives at all:

adagio	slowly
volentieri	willingly
altrimenti	otherwise

4 A small number of adverbs, for example the following, end in -oni:

bocconi	flat on one's face
carponi	on all fours
ginocchioni	on one's knees
a tentoni	feeling one's way
a cavalcioni	astride

5 Certain adjectives in their masculine singular form may be used instead of adverbs:

parlare piano	to speak softly
vedere chiaro	to see clearly
lavorare sodo	to work hard
abitare vicino	to live nearby
piovere forte	to rain heavily
tagliare corto	to cut short
stare fermo	to stand still

6 Alternative ways of forming adverbs:

a) An adverb can be replaced by an adverbial phrase, for example in modo, in maniera + adjective:

agire in modo strano	rispondere in maniera sgarbata
to act strangely	to reply rudely

b) Preposition + noun:

con calma	calmly
con eleganza	elegantly
senza paura	fearlessly
senza difficoltà	easily
a malincuore	reluctantly
in fretta	hastily

c) Other adverbial phrases (*see also* pp 72-3):

di buon grado	willingly
ad occhio nudo	with the naked eye

B ADVERBS OF TIME

These answer the question 'when?' Here are some common examples:

oggi	today
ieri	yesterday
domani	tomorrow
stamattina	this morning

stasera	this evening
stanotte	last night, tonight
ora, adesso	now
allora, poi	then
subito	immediately, at once
prima	before
dopo	after, afterwards
spesso	often
sempre	always
presto	soon, early, quickly
tardi	late
già	already
ancora	still, yet, again
finora	until now, so far
ormai, oramai	by now, by then, by this time
infine	in the end, finally
intanto	meanwhile
mai	ever, never

scrivimi presto
write to me soon

muoviamoci, presto!
let's move, quickly!

aspetta ancora una settimana
wait another week

non sei mai a casa
you're never at home

mi sono alzato presto
I got up early

sta ancora mangiando
he/she's still eating

non sono ancora pronto
I'm not ready yet

sei mai stato a Milano?
have you ever been to Milan?

Note that some adverbs of time like prima and dopo are also used as prepositions:

me l'ha confessato dopo
he/she confessed it to me
  afterwards *(adverb)*

telefonerò dopo le vacanze
I'll call after the holidays
  (preposition)

For adverbial phrases of time, see also pp 72-3.

C ADVERBS OF PLACE

These answer the questions 'where?' Here are some common examples:

qui, qua	here
lì, là	there
qua e là	here and there
sotto	under, below
sopra	up, on, above
fuori	out, outside
dentro	in, inside
su	on, up
giù	down
quassù	up here
quaggiù	down here
lassù	up there
laggiù	down there
lontano	far away
vicino	near, nearby
dietro	behind
(d)avanti	in front
indietro	behind
intorno	around
dappertutto	everywhere
dovunque	everywhere
altrove	elsewhere

avanti!
come in!

su le mani!
hands up!

gli uffici sono sopra
the offices are above

c'è scritto sopra il mio nome
my name is written on it

qua sopra ci sono i dizionari
the dictionaries are up here

c'è una farmacia qui vicino
there's a chemist near here

Note that some adverbs of place, such as sopra, sotto, su, dentro, fuori, davanti, dietro, intorno *etc* also function as prepositions:

guarda su!   **il libro è sul tavolo**
look up *(adverb)*   the book is on the table *(preposition)*

Note too that adverbial particles ci (here, there), vi (here, there) and ne (from there) are dealt with in the Pronoun section (*see* pp 83-9).

D ADVERBS OF QUANTITY AND INTENSITY

This category answers the question 'to what extent?' or 'with how much intensity?' Here are some common examples:

quanto*	how much
molto*	much, a lot, very
assai	very
poco*	little
un po'	a little
tanto*	so much, a lot, very
abbastanza	enough
parecchio*	quite a lot
troppo*	too much
così	so
talmente	so
nulla, niente	nothing
appena	hardly, scarcely, just
almeno	at least
alquanto	somewhat
più	more
meno	less
solo, soltanto	only
altrettanto	as much, so much
quasi	almost

sono appena partiti they have just left	**lo vedo appena** I can hardly see him
quanto costa? how much does it cost?	**li vedo molto poco** I very seldom see them

* These adverbs must not be confused with the corresponding adjectives or pronouns:

ho mangiato molto I've eaten a lot *(adverb)*	**ne ho mangiati molti** I've eaten many of them *(pronoun)*
ho mangiato molti biscotti I've eaten a lot of biscuits *(adjective)*	

E ADVERBS OF AFFIRMATION, NEGATION AND DOUBT

1 Affirmation

sì	yes
certo, certamente	certainly
sicuro, sicuramente	certainly, surely
senz'altro	certainly
senza dubbio	undoubtedly
veramente	really, truly
davvero	really, truly
appunto	precisely

hai fame? – sì are you hungry? – yes(, I am)	**vi piace la musica? – sì** do you like music? – yes(, we do)
ti piace davvero? do you really like it?	

2 Negation

no	no
non	not
nemmeno	not even
mai	never
niente, nulla	nothing
non ... affatto	not ... at all

è vero? – no	**no, non ci credo!**
is it true? – no(, it's not)	no, I don't believe it!
non gli ho nemmeno parlato	**non ci sono mai stato**
I didn't even speak to him	I've never been there
hai letto questo libro? – no	
have you read this book? – no(, I haven't)	
non ho affatto fame	**sei stanco? – niente affatto**
I'm not hungry at all	are you tired? – not at all

For further treatment of negative expressions see **pp 255–9.**

3 Doubt

forse	perhaps, maybe
probabilmente	probably
quasi	almost
perché	why
eventualmente	if necessary, if need be

eventualmente verrò domani
I'll come tomorrow, if need be

F COMPARATIVE AND SUPERLATIVE OF ADVERBS

1 For adverbs of manner (except the ones ending in -oni), and a few adverbs of time and place, the formation of the comparative and superlative parallels that of adjectives. The superlative is formed by adding -issimo to the stem of the adverb; if the adverb ends with -mente, then -issima + mente are added:

ADVERB	COMPARATIVE	SUPERLATIVE
lentamente	più lentamente	lentissimamente
slowly	more slowly	very slowly
spesso	più spesso	spessissimo
often	more often	very often
lontano	più lontano	lontanissimo
far	further	very far

ha reagito più rapidamente del solito
he/she has reacted more quickly than usual

oggi finiremo tardissimo
today we'll finish very late

2 Irregular comparatives and superlatives

ADVERB	COMPARATIVE	SUPERLATIVE
bene	meglio	ottimamente/benissimo
well	better	very well
male	peggio	pessimamente/
		malissimo
badly	worse	very badly
molto	più	moltissimo
much, very	more	very much
poco	meno	pochissimo
little	less	very little
grandemente	maggiormente	massimamente
greatly	more	most, mostly

3 Use

a) As seen in the above tables the Italian adverbial superlative is normally used to express the idea of 'very ...'

b) Whereas it is common in English to form constructions of the type 'he trained the hardest' or 'this printer prints the fastest', Italian will tend to use a different type of construction to express the same idea:

di tutte le stampanti questa è quella che stampa più velocemente
of all the printers this one prints the fastest

sicuramente fuma meno di tutti gli altri/rispetto agli altri è quello che fuma meno
compared with the others he definitely smokes the least

le persone arrivate per prime sono quelle che sono rimaste più a lungo
the people who arrived first also stayed the longest

> **l'automobile che ha dato la miglior prestazione**
> the car which performed (the) best in the trials

c) The superlative may be expressed in other ways:

  i) by placing **molto** (very), **assai** (very) or **estremamente** (extremely) in front of the adverb

  guidava assai lentamente
  he/she drove very slowly

  ii) in a limited number of cases, by duplication of the adjective or adverb:

pian(o) piano	**lento lento**
very slowly, very softly	very slowly

d) Superlative with **il più/meno … possible** (as … as possible):

  vorrei andare in vacanza il più lontano possibile
  I'd like to go on holiday as far away as possible

  scrivimi il più presto possibile
  write to me as soon as possible

e) Comparative with **meno** (less):

  ci ha telefonato meno spesso quest'anno
  he/she has phoned us less often this year

G ADDITIONAL POINTS

1 Adverbial Phrases

Commonly used expressions such as the following have an adverbial function:

sempre (di) più	more and more
sempre (di) meno	less and less
sempre più veloce	faster and faster
più o meno	more or less

al più presto	as quickly as possible, as soon as possible
di bene in meglio	better and better
di male in peggio	worse and worse
meno male	thank goodness, just as well
meglio/peggio che mai	so much the better/worse
alla meglio	as best one can
di tanto in tanto	every so often
ogni tanto	every so often
d'ora in poi	from now on
a poco a poco	little by little
di buon'ora	early
ad un tratto	suddenly
all'improvviso	unexpectedly
all'italiana	Italian-style

2 Suffixes

In rare cases adverbs may be modified by suffixes:

bene	benino	benone
well	tolerably well	extremely well
male	maluccio	
badly	not too well	
poco	pochino	
little	rather little	

ho mangiato poco	ho mangiato pochino
I ate little	I ate rather little

3 Position of Adverbs

a) Although the position of adverbs may sometimes be varied for reasons of emphasis or expressiveness, they normally follow the verb they modify:

ci ha salutato molto gentilmente   **abito lontano**
he/she greeted us very warmly   I live far away

Note the position of the following common adverbs of time when the verb is in a compound tense:

te l'ho già detto mille volte
I have already told you a thousand times

non ho mai visto una cosa simile!
I've never seen such a thing!

b) When the adverb modifies an adjective or another adverb it usually precedes it:

sono arrivato molto tardi
I arrived very late

il suo comportamento è stato poco dignitoso
his/her behaviour was not very dignified

5 PRONOUNS

PERSONAL PRONOUNS

There are four categories of personal pronouns:

❏ subject pronouns
❏ object pronouns
❏ disjunctive pronouns
❏ reflexive pronouns

For reflexive pronouns see p 127.

A SUBJECT PRONOUNS

1 Forms

PERSON	SINGULAR		PLURAL	
1st	io	I	noi	we
2nd	tu	you	voi	you
3rd	lui (egli, esso)	he, it	loro (essi)	they *(masc)*
	lei (ella, essa)	she, it	loro (esse)	they *(fem)*
polite forms	lei	you	loro	you

2 Use

a) tu and voi are the singular and plural forms used when speaking to relatives, friends, children and animals.

b) lui, lei and loro are now the most commonly used third person pronouns, particularly in spoken Italian. The forms egli and ella, as well as essi and esse, are now mainly found in the written language. esso and essa are used to refer to animals, inanimate objects or abstractions, but are frequently omitted.

c) Polite forms are used when speaking to an older or unknown person:

   i) **lei** is the singular polite form of address. **loro** is the plural, although the **voi** form is now used in all but the most formal contexts.

   lei and **loro** may be written with initial capitals, particularly in formal letters.

   lei and **loro** always take the third person singular and plural forms of the verb respectively:

   lei è veramente fortunato/a!   **come loro desiderano**
   you're really lucky!   as you prefer

   ii) **voi** is used as a singular polite form in some regions of Italy and is common in commercial correspondence.

Note

The following expression is particularly associated with the use of the informal second person or formal (polite) third person pronoun forms:

dare del tu / dare del lei
to use the 'tu'/'lei' form

diamoci del tu
let's use the 'tu' form

---

d) The subject pronouns may be followed by **stesso** (which agrees with its subject) in order to express 'myself', 'yourself' etc:

   io stesso ho parlato con la preside
   I myself have spoken to the headmistress

e) Italian uses subject pronouns with the verb 'to be' in the following type of construction:

   chi è? – sono io/siamo noi
   who is it? – it's me/it's us

This may also be used without a verb:

chi? io?
who? me?

3 Omission of Pronouns

The subject pronouns are frequently omitted in Italian as the verb endings are often sufficient to indicate the person:

non voglio
I don't want to

che cosa avete detto?
what did you say?

They may be used, however:

a) For clarity, eg with the singular persons of the present subjunctive which have the same form:

hanno paura che io abbia perso le chiavi
they're afraid I've lost the keys

b) For emphasis:

pago io
I'm paying

tu che ne pensi?
what do *you* think of it?

pensaci tu!
you think about it!

me l'hanno detto loro
they told me

c) For contrast:

io vado in piscina, lui invece rimane a casa
I'm going to the swimming pool but he's staying at home

d) Subject pronouns must not be omitted after adverbs such as anche, neppure *etc*:

anche voi dovete provare
you must try too

vengo anch'io!
I'm coming too!

neppure noi abbiamo voglia di vederli
we don't want to see them either

B OBJECT PRONOUNS

These are also known as conjunctive pronouns or weak pronouns.
They cannot stand by themselves but must be used in conjunction
with a verb. Object pronouns include:

- ❏ direct object pronouns
- ❏ indirect object pronouns
- ❏ the particles ne and ci (vi)

1 Forms

PERSON	DIRECT		INDIRECT	
1st sing	mi	me	mi	to me
2nd sing	ti	you	ti	to you
3rd sing	lo	him, it	gli	to him, to it
	la	her, it	le	to her, to it
1st plural	ci	us	ci	to us
2nd plural	vi	you	vi	to you
3rd plural	li	them *(masc)*	loro	to them *(masc)*
	le	them *(fem)*	loro	to them *(fem)*
polite forms				
sing	la	you *(masc, fem)*	le	to you *(masc, fem)*
plural	li	you *(masc)*	loro	to you *(masc, fem)*
	le	you *(fem)*		

non lo conosco   **vi hanno risposto?**
I don't know him   have they replied to you?

2 Use

a) lo is often used in Italian as a neuter pronoun which may be
   omitted when translating into English:

   Gigi si è sposato – lo so!
   Gigi got married – I know!

It may also substitute for an entire phrase in order to avoid repetition:

preferite andare in treno? – sì, lo preferiamo
do you prefer going by train? – yes, we do

b) In spoken Italian gli is tending to replace loro to mean 'to them' (of course it can also mean 'to him'):

gli ho detto di sbrigarsi
I told him/them to hurry up

c) Elision of pronouns is common with third person singular direct object pronouns in the perfect and pluperfect tenses but may also occur with the first and second persons singular; the latter also tend to elide when followed by a verb beginning with i:

m'hanno fatto ridere tanto   **l'ho visto due volte**
they made me laugh such a lot   I saw him twice

t'interessa vedere di nuovo quel film?
are you interested in seeing that film again?

l'abbiamo invitata all'ultimo momento
we invited her at the last minute

But with third person plural direct object pronouns there is no elision:

li ho visti due volte
I saw them twice

le abbiamo invitate all'ultimo momento
we invited them at the last minute

d) Certain verbs requiring a direct object in English must be followed by an indirect object in Italian:

le telefoneremo   **credigli!**
we'll phone her   believe him/them!

Certain verbs requiring the indirect object in English must be followed by a direct object in Italian:

ascoltami   **l'aspetterò all'angolo**
listen to me   I'll wait for him/her at the corner

Particular care must be taken in Italian with verbs which also require an indirect pronoun in English, although the fact that one pronoun *is* an indirect pronoun may not be obvious:

gli ho mandato un assegno
I sent him/them a cheque = I sent a cheque to him/them

This is also the case with the following verbs:

comprare	to buy
dare	to give
dire	to tell
mostrare	to show
offrire	to offer
prestare	to lend
vendere	to sell

le ho comprato un paio di scarpe   **prestagli dieci euro**
I bought her a pair of shoes   lend him/them ten euros

3 Agreement

In compound tenses, the participle always agrees with the preceding third person direct object pronoun:

hai già scritto la lettera? – sì, l'ho scritta ieri
have you written the letter already? – yes, I wrote it yesterday

avete chiesto le informazioni? – sì, le abbiamo già chieste
have you asked for the information? – yes, we've already asked for it

Agreement is optional in the case of the first and second person:

ti ho visto in centro ieri, Silvia   **non ci hanno visto**
ti ho vista in centro ieri, Silvia   **non ci hanno visti/e**
I saw you in town yesterday, Silvia   they didn't see us

4 Position

a) All object pronouns precede a finite verb (the auxiliary in the case of compound tenses) *except* the third person plural indirect object pronoun loro ('to them', 'to you' *polite*):

gli ho dato uno schiaffo
I gave him a slap

non ci hanno mai incoraggiati
they have never encouraged us

avevo dato loro il mio numero di telefono
I had given them my phone number

Note that the negative non precedes the pronouns.

b) In the cases outlined below, however, the object pronouns are added to the end of the verb form:

i) with infinitives, in which case the final e is dropped:

sono venuto per aiutarti	**ha continuato a guardarla**
I've come to help you	he went on looking at her

va' a dargli la buona notizia
go and tell him/them the good news

ii) with modal verbs plus an infinitive there are two possibilities:

non voglio vederlo più	**posso farle una domanda?**
non lo voglio più vedere	**le posso fare una domanda?**
I don't want to see him any more	may I ask you a question?

iii) with gerunds:

lo stava osservando	**osservandolo attentamente**
stava osservandolo	observing him/it closely
he/she was observing him/it	

avendoli comprati, adesso vogliamo goderceli
having bought them, we now want to enjoy them

iv) with past participles standing alone:

finitolo	**parlatogli**
having finished it	having spoken to him

v) with informal imperatives:

perdonami	**scrivetelo**	**dimmi**
forgive me	write it	tell me

fallo subito	**ascoltiamoli**
do it right away	let's listen to them

For the position of pronouns with both formal and informal imperatives, and for the doubling of consonants in the last two examples above, see also **pp 161-2.**

Note that with the negative imperative two pronoun positions are possible:

non leggerlo
non lo leggere
don't read it

vi) with ecco:

eccolo!	**eccoci!**	**eccomi!**	**eccoli!**
here he/it is!	here we are!	here I am!	here they are!

Note that in all the above cases the third person plural indirect pronoun loro follows the verb and remains separate from it:

ho voluto vendere loro la casa
I wanted to sell them the house

avendo insegnato loro come si pronuncia questa parola ...
having taught them how this word is pronounced ...

parla loro
speak to them

5 Order of object pronouns

When direct and indirect pronouns are used together, the indirect precedes the direct and the following changes occur; the indirect object and reflexive pronouns mi, ti, ci, vi and the third person singular and plural reflexive pronoun si become me, te, ce, ve and se:

me lo	me la	me li	me le
te lo	te la	te li	te le
se lo	se la	se li	se le
ce lo	ce la	ce li	ce le
ve lo	ve la	ve li	ve le
se lo	se la	se li	se le

me lo presterai?
will you lend it to me?

ce li hanno presentati
they introduced them to us

me l'ha detto
he/she told me

se lo ripete spesso
he often repeats it to himself

gli and le (also in the polite form) become glie- and combine with the direct object pronoun to give:

glielo, gliela, glieli and gliele

glielo/a/i/e Note that these words can have a range of meanings:

glielo manderò
I'll send it to him/her/them (*masc or fem*)/you (*polite form, sing or plur, masc or fem*)

gliel'ho sempre detto
I have always told him/her/them/you that

glieli abbiamo già inviati
we have already sent them to him/her/them/you

vorrei regalarglielo
I would like to give it to him/her/them/you

For the position of object pronouns, and in particular of loro, see also pp 81–82.

 C THE PARTICLE ne

Ne (and also ci (vi)) has both an adverbial and a pronominal function. In neither case, however, can the particle stand by itself.

Instead it must be used in conjunction with a verb in the same way as object pronouns.

In its pronominal function *ne* has a range of meanings including 'of it/him/her/them', 'about it/him/her/them', 'of this/that', 'some' and 'any'.

1 Use

a) It is particularly associated with the preposition *di*:

   i) to replace *di* + noun or pronoun:

     che cosa sai di questa faccenda? – non ne so nulla
     what do you know about this affair? – I don't know anything about it

     avete bisogno della macchina stasera? – no, non ne abbiamo bisogno
     do you need the car this evening? – no, we don't need it

     cosa pensi di Gianni? – che ne pensi?
     what do you think of Gianni? – what do you think of him?

     non me ne importa niente
     I couldn't care less about it

   ii) to replace some clauses introduced by *di*. Many Italian verbs can be followed by the preposition *di*, for example: *dimenticarsi* (to forget), *rallegrarsi* (to be pleased), *accorgersi* (to notice), *rendersi conto* (to realize), *pentirsi* (to regret), *servirsi* (to use) *etc* (*see also pp 207-9*):

     mi sono dimenticato di dar da mangiare al gatto – me ne sono dimenticato
     I forgot to feed the cat – I forgot about it

     Lucia ha agito da sciocca, ma adesso se ne pente
     Lucia acted like an idiot, but now she regrets it

b) It is also used to replace the partitive (*del, della, dei etc*):

     hai comprato dei libri di Calvino? – no, non ne ho comprati
     did you buy any books by Calvino? – no, I didn't buy any

c'è ancora del denaro da spendere? – no, non ce n'è più
is there any money left to spend? – no, there isn't any left

c) **ne** is essential with numerals and adjectives of quantity when the noun is not repeated and a verb is used. It should be noted that whereas in the following Italian examples **ne** is essential, it will not usually be translated into English:

quanti anni hai? – ne ho diciassette
how old are you? – I'm seventeen

che belle pesche! ne comprerò un chilo
what wonderful peaches! I'll buy a kilo

come mi piacciono questi cioccolatini! ne ho mangiati tantissimi!
I really love these chocolates! I've eaten lots of them!

d) In its adverbial function **ne** means 'from there/here' and is associated with the preposition **da**:

è facile entrare nel labirinto – il difficile è uscirne
it is easy to get into the maze – the difficulty lies in getting out of it

vattene!
go away!

2 Position

a) **ne** precedes the verb except in the cases described in B 4 b):

ne hai parlato col padrone? – no, non ne ho ancora parlato con lui
have you spoken to the boss about it? – no, I haven't spoken to him about it yet

b) Where it is used in conjunction with an indirect object pronoun or a reflexive pronoun it takes second place:

non me ne intendo molto
I don't know much about it

eccone due!
here are two of them!

me ne andrò domani
I'm going away tomorrow

vorrei andarmene
I'd like to go away

te ne parlerò domani
I'll speak to you about it tomorrow

posso parlarvene un attimo?
may I speak to you about it for a moment?

parliamogliene, se vuoi
let's talk to him/her/them about it, if you want

3 Agreement

ne can agree with the past participle only in its partitive use (*see also* pp 174-5):

ho bevuto della birra – ne hai bevuta anche tu?
I've had some beer – have you had some too?

 D THE PARTICLE ci (vi)

ci and vi are object pronouns, but they can also be used as adverbs. vi is identical to ci but is used rather less, particularly in spoken Italian. The choice between the two is usually made on phonetic or stylistic grounds. For instance, in order to avoid alliteration in a phrase such as vi vado (I'm going there), the form ci vado is preferred.

In their pronominal function ci and vi could have a range of different meanings including 'to it/them/this/that', 'of it/them/this/that', 'about it/them/this/that', 'on it/them/this/that', *etc.*

1 Use

a) They are particularly associated with the preposition a (to):

  i) to replace a + noun or pronoun:

   crede alle promesse fatte dalle autorità? – no, non ci credo
   do you believe in the promises made by the authorities? – no, I don't believe in them
   pensi all'avvenire? – sì, ci penso spesso
   do you think about the future? – yes, I often think about it

ii) to replace **a** + verb:

**sei riuscito a portare quella valigia alla stazione? – no, non ci sono
riuscito, ho dovuto prendere un taxi**
did you manage to carry that suitcase to the station? – no, I didn't,
I had to get a taxi

provate a spiegarglielo più chiaramente – ci proveremo!
try to explain it to him more clearly – we'll try to

iii) to replace other constructions:

ci puoi contare	**ci puoi scommettere!**
you can depend on it	you can bet on it!

ci penseremo domani
we'll think about it tomorrow

dice di non saperlo, ma io non ci credo
he says he doesn't know, but I don't believe it

mi dispiace, non so che farci!
I'm sorry, I don't know what to do about it!

b) In their adverbial function **ci** and **vi** mean 'there' and 'to there'
and are associated principally with the preposition **a** but also
with **in** and **su**:

sei mai stato a Pisa? – sì, ci sono stato diverse volte
have you ever been to Pisa? – yes, I have been there a number of times

ci siamo rimasti due mesi
we stayed there for two months

a che ora vai a scuola? – ci vado alle otto e mezzo
what time do you go to school? – I go at half past eight

ti piacerebbe vivere in Italia? – sì, mi piacerebbe viverci
would you like to live in Italy? – yes, I would like to live there

2 Position

Like **ne** and the other object pronouns, **ci** and **vi** precede the verb
except in the cases described in section B 4 b) above:

ci andrò domani	**andiamoci stasera**
I'll go there tomorrow	let's go there this evening

ci è già stata altre volte
she has already been there on other occasions

In combination with other pronouns, ci and vi precede lo, la, li, le and ne and change their form to ce and ve:

ce l'ho messo io!
I put it there

mi dispiace, non ce ne sono più
I'm sorry, there aren't any left

Note

- ci and vi follow mi and ti:

  mi ci troverai ogni sabato sera
  you will find me there every Saturday evening

- Alternative modes of expression, such as the adverbs of place lì or là, may be substituted:

  mi troverai lì ogni sabato sera
  you will find me there every Saturday evening

3 With reflexives

When using ci and vi with a reflexive verb their relation to the reflexive pronoun varies as follows:

> **mi ci abituo** (I'm getting used to it)
> **ti ci abitui** (you're getting used to it)
> **ci si abitua** (one's/he's/she's/you're getting used to it)
> *vi ci abituiamo (we're getting used to it)
> **vi ci abituate** (you're getting used to it)
> **ci si abituano** (they're/you're getting used to it)

*vi is used here to avoid the repetitive ci ci (although this is rare).

Note the following uses of ci:

hai il passaporto? – sì, ce l'ho
have you got your passport? – yes, I have

avete tre euro, per caso? – ci dispiace, non ce li abbiamo
have you got three euros by any chance? – no, sorry, we haven't

**quanto tempo ci vuole per andare a Trieste in macchina? – ci vogliono
due ore**
how long does it take to drive to Trieste? – it takes two hours

 E DISJUNCTIVE PRONOUNS

Unlike the conjunctive pronouns studied above, disjunctive
pronouns are not so strongly linked to the verb. They are
particularly associated with prepositions.

1 Forms

PERSON	SINGULAR		PLURAL	
1st	me	me	noi	us
2nd	te	you	voi	you
3rd	lui	him	loro	them *(masc)*
	lei	her	loro	them *(fem)*
	esso/a	it	essi/e	them
	sé	himself/herself	sé	themselves
		yourself		yourselves
		itself		
polite forms	lei	you	loro	you

vieni con noi   **tocca a te**
come with us   it's your turn

For use of the formal and informal pronoun forms, see **subject
pronouns** *p 75.*

2 Use

a) When the verb has two direct or indirect objects or one pronoun
and one noun, the disjunctive pronouns must be used in place
of conjunctive pronouns:

ho invitato lui ma non lei
I invited him but not her

hanno fornito le informazioni necessarie a noi ma non a loro
they provided us but not them with the necessary information

sono piaciuti enormemente a me e a mia sorella
my sister and I liked them enormously

b) For emphasis in place of a conjunctive pronoun – compare:

non mi hanno detto niente
they haven't told me anything

a me non hanno detto niente
they haven't told *me* anything

non mi sembra brutto
it doesn't seem ugly to me

a me non sembra brutto
it doesn't seem ugly to *me*

c) With prepositions, including prepositions following verbs:

andiamo con loro
let's go with them

secondo noi, lui ha torto
in our opinion he's wrong

fra me e te
between you and me

dipende da lei
it depends on her/you

sono venuti incontro a noi
they came to meet us

è venuta da me ieri sera
she came to my house yesterday evening

pensa solo a sé
he/she thinks only of himself/herself

d) With comparisons:

tu sei più simpatica di lui
you are nicer than him

lui è meno esigente di noi
he's less demanding than us

loro sono bravi quanto voi
they're as good as you

e) With expressions of the following type:

povero me
poor me

beata te
lucky you

F THE IMPERSONAL PRONOUN si

As an impersonal pronoun, si is the equivalent of the English 'one'
(or more commonly 'we' or 'they' or 'people'). It is followed by
the third person singular of the verb. It has, however, a number
of special features which merit close study. In the examples which
follow, si will be used only with intransitive verbs (or with verbs
used intransitively); *for its passive function with transitive verbs,
see* p 179:

a) At its simplest si operates like a subject pronoun:

non si sa mai   **si va via?**
one never knows/you never know   shall we leave?

di solito si mangia all'una
we normally eat at one o'clock

ogni giorno si lavora dalle otto alle due
every day we work from eight till two

b) When followed by the verbs essere, restare, rimanere, stare and
diventare, si requires a plural adjective:

quando si è giovani, non si accetta sempre di essere criticati
when one is young, one cannot always take criticism

si rimane sempre soddisfatti in questo ristorante
one is always satisfied in this restaurant

c) With reflexive verbs si changes to ci in order to avoid repetition:

durante la settimana ci si alza di buon'ora
during the week we/you get up early

non ci si rende sempre conto del pericolo
one does not always realize the danger

d) In compound tenses when using si *all* verbs must be conjugated
with essere, including those which normally take avere. Verbs

normally conjugated with **essere** will have a plural past participle:

si è studiato tutta la settimana
we've been studying all week

si è arrivati a Siena alle sette di sera
we arrived in Siena at seven in the evening

non si è capito cosa voleva
we didn't understand what he/she wanted

ci si è abituati al nuovo orario
we got used to the new timetable

e) The position of the pronouns with **si** is as follows: all pronouns precede **si** except **ne** which follows. In the latter case **si** changes to **se**:

lo si dice un po' dappertutto
people are saying it just about everywhere

se ne discute ogni tanto   **ci si può andare a piedi**
we/they discuss it every so often   you can go there on foot

Note that **si** may be replaced by the indefinite pronoun **uno**, which does not have the special features of the former but which is also less frequently used in Italian:

uno si trova bene in questa pensione
one is quite comfortable in this guesthouse

G POSSESSIVE ADJECTIVES AND PRONOUNS

1 Forms

The forms of possessive adjectives and pronouns are identical in Italian. They are always accompanied by the definite article except in certain clearly defined cases shown below. They agree in number and gender with the object or the person 'possessed'.

SINGULAR		PLURAL		
MASCULINE	**FEMININE**	**MASCULINE**	**FEMININE**	
il mio	la mia	i miei	le mie	my, mine
il tuo	la tua	i tuoi	le tue	your, yours
il suo	la sua	i suoi	le sue	his, her, hers, its
il nostro	la nostra	i nostri	le nostre	our, ours
il vostro	la vostra	i vostri	le vostre	your, yours
il loro	la loro	i loro	le loro	their, theirs
polite forms				
il suo	la sua	i suoi	le sue	your, yours *(sing)*
il loro	la loro	i loro	le loro	your, yours *(plural)*

il mio cane
my dog

la sua sciarpa
his/her/your scarf

i suoi vestiti
his/her/your clothes

le tue impressioni
your impressions

il suo conto, signore
your bill, Sir

i loro affari
their/your business

Note

- The possessive forms associated with the polite forms of address are, like the latter, sometimes written with an initial capital letter:

  la Sua lettera del 12 aprile
  your letter of 12th April

- loro is invariable:

  la loro automobile
  their/your car

  i loro amici
  their/your friends

- As the pronoun voi is now generally used instead of the polite form loro in all but the most formal contexts, so the possessive il vostro now usually replaces il loro.

2 Use of the possessive adjective

a) The possessive adjective is repeated before each noun and agrees with it:

i tuoi blue-jeans e le tue scarpe sono bagnati
your jeans and your shoes are soaking wet

b) Where ambiguities arise concerning the third person possessives, alternative forms may be employed. For instance,

la sua giacca
his/her/your jacket

may be expressed more clearly by using the disjunctive pronouns (*see* p 89):

la giacca di lui　　　　　　　　　**la giacca di lei**
his jacket　　　　　　　　　　　　　her jacket

The adjective proprio may also be used:

Mario andò via con Paolo e prese la propria automobile
Mario left with Paolo and took his own car

c) In Italian the possessive adjective itself is often omitted in cases where the identity of the possessor is already clear from the context:

metti il cappotto　　　　　　　　**hanno chinato la testa**
put your coat on　　　　　　　　　　they bent their heads

ha gli occhi azzurri
his/her/your eyes are blue

d) Omission of the definite article with the possessive:

i) with family relationships in the singular, with all possessive adjectives except loro:

mia sorella　　　　　　　　　　　**nostro cugino**
my sister　　　　　　　　　　　　　　our cousin

il loro genero
their/your son-in-law

In the plural, however, the article is not omitted:

le mie sorelle
my sisters

i tuoi cugini
your cousins

Note

The forms babbo (dad), mamma (mum), nonno (grandpa) and nonna (grandma) may be found with or without the definite article (mio babbo or il mio babbo).

However, if the possessive is used with another adjective or if the noun has a suffix, then the definite article is not omitted:

il tuo fratellino
your little brother

il nostro vecchio padre
our old father

la mia sorella sposata
my married sister

la mia sorella maggiore
my eldest sister

ii) with certain prepositional phrases:

a mio parere
in my opinion

a vostra disposizione
at your disposal

iii) when the adjective is placed after the noun:
   ❏ with the vocative case:

   Dio mio!
   my God!

   ❏ with certain set phrases:

   è colpa mia
   it's my fault

   casa mia
   my house

   non sono affari vostri
   it's none of your business

   fa sempre tutto di testa sua
   he/she does everything he/she pleases

e) Instead of the definite article other parts of speech may be found in conjunction with the possessive adjective:

una mia amica
a friend of mine

due miei amici
two friends of mine

molti miei coetanei
many of my age group

quel mio collega
that colleague of mine

3 Use of the possessive pronoun

In the following examples possessive adjectives are used in the first part of the sentence, and possessive pronouns in the second part. The latter simply substitute for the missing noun:

ho dimenticato il mio dizionario; prestami il tuo
I've forgotten my dictionary; lend me yours

mia sorella si è laureata l'anno scorso, e la tua?
my sister graduated last year, what about yours?

è carina la tua gonna, mi piace più della mia
your skirt is really nice, I like it better than mine

la loro macchina somiglia molto alla nostra
their car looks a lot like ours

> ## Note
>
> • The article is sometimes omitted when the pronoun is preceded by **essere** but there is a slight difference in meaning:
>
> **questa borsa è la mia**
> this is my bag *(one of a number)*
>
> **questa borsa è mia**
> this is my bag *(my property)*
>
> • When a possessive pronoun refers to two preceding nouns of different gender, the masculine form predominates:
>
> **questa chiave e questo passaporto sono miei**
> this key and this passport are mine

H **INDEFINITE PRONOUNS AND ADJECTIVES**

These fall into three categories:

❑ words functioning only as indefinite pronouns
❑ words functioning only as indefinite adjectives
❑ words functioning both as indefinite pronouns and adjectives

1 Indefinite pronouns

The following cannot be used with a noun and are found only in the singular:

uno/una	one
ognuno/ognuna	each one, everyone
qualcuno/qualcuna	someone, anyone
qualcosa	something, anything
chiunque	anyone
nulla/niente	nothing

se uno arriva con qualche minuto di ritardo ...
if one arrives a minute or two late ...

ognuno deve pensare alle proprie responsabilità
everyone must think about their own responsibilities

qualcuno è venuto a trovarti ma non so chi
somebody came looking for you but I don't know who

vuoi qualcosa da bere?   c'è qualcosa di nuovo?
do you want something to drink?   is there anything new?

chiunque è capace di usare un computer
anybody can use a computer

non ne so niente/nulla di preciso
I don't know anything specific about it

grazie mille! – di niente!
thanks a lot! – don't mention it!

Note the following points:

i) uno does in fact appear in the plural when it is followed by altri/e. In this case it is always preceded by the definite article:

gli uni vogliono andar via, gli altri vogliono restare qui
some want to go, (the) others want to stay here

It has a reciprocal meaning in the phrase l'un l'altro used with a reflexive verb:

si aiutano l'un l'altro
they're helping one another

However, with other verbs a preposition must be added:

discutevano l'uno con l'altro
they were arguing with one another

ii) niente, when it follows the verb, requires a double negation (*see also* p 258):

non è successo niente
nothing happened

Note the following exception to the above rule:

niente lo fermerà
nothing will stop him

2 Indefinite adjectives

These must accompany a noun. All five are invariable.

ogni	each, every
qualche	some, a few
qualsiasi	any, any at all, some ... or other
qualunque	any, any at all, some ... or other
altrui	another's, of other people

Note the following points:

i) ogni is always used with singular nouns:

ogni giorno　　　　　　　　　**ogni madre**
every day　　　　　　　　　　　every mother

Observe the usage with numerals:

vado dal medico ogni sei mesi
I go to the doctor every six months

ii) qualche is always used with a singular noun and only with
those nouns which could have a plural:

l'ho già incontrata qualche volta
I've already met her a few times

al largo si vedeva qualche barca a vela
offshore one could see a few sailing boats

For those nouns which do not have a plural, an expression
such as un po' di must be used:

un po' di latte
some milk

iii) qualsiasi and qualunque are used with singular nouns and are
interchangeable. When they follow the noun, they have the
meaning of 'any at all', 'it doesn't matter which':

darei qualsiasi cosa per assistere alla partita
I would give anything to see the match

mi dia un giornale qualsiasi
give me any newspaper at all

è un uomo qualsiasi
he is just an ordinary man

pagherebbe qualunque prezzo per acquistare quel quadro
he/she'd pay any price to get that painting

qualunque cosa dicessi, non ti crederei
whatever you said, I wouldn't believe you

iv) altrui follows the noun:

non toccare la roba altrui
don't touch other people's things

3 Indefinite pronouns or adjectives

nessuno/a	no one, no
ciascuno/a	each one, everyone, each
alcuno/a/i/e	some
altro/a/i/e	another, other
troppo/a/i/e	too many, too much
molto/a/i/e	many, much
poco/poca/pochi/poche	few
tanto/a/i/e	so many, so much
quanto/a/i/e	as many, as much, how many, how much
parecchio/chia/chi/chie	several
tale/i	such
tutto/a/i/e	all, every
certo/a/i/e	certain

The rules for the omission of the o in the indefinite adjectives
nessuno, ciascuno and alcuno are the same as for uno, *see* p 20.

quest'anno nessuno ha celebrato la festa
this year no one celebrated the festival

nessuna donna accetterebbe di essere trattata così
no woman would accept being treated like that

ho dato un regalo a ciascuno di loro
I gave each of them a present

non fa altro che piangere
he/she does nothing but cry

si deve trovare un'altra soluzione
another solution must be found

a molti è parsa una decisione sbagliata
to many people it seemed like the wrong decision

molti spettatori sono stati feriti
many spectators were injured

pochi s'interessano a quell'argomento
few people are interested in that subject

siamo arrivati a casa poco tempo fa
we got home a little while ago

parecchi erano già andati via
several people had already left

mi sono rimaste parecchie cose da fare
I have several things left to do

c'è un tale che l'aspetta in ufficio
there's someone waiting for you in the office

una tale spiegazione non soddisferà mai il pubblico
such an explanation will never satisfy the public

a quell'incrocio succede un incidente tutte le settimane
every week there's an accident at that crossroads

non tutti possono permettersi il lusso di viaggiare
not everyone can afford to travel

Note the following points:

i) alcuno can be used both in the singular and in the plural, but if it occurs in an affirmative sentence it must be in the plural:

ho letto alcuni libri di Calvino
I've read some books by Calvino

non ho alcun dubbio
I have no doubt(s)

alcuni piatti regionali sono facili da preparare
some regional dishes are easy to prepare

alcuni accettano la nuova tecnologia, altri no
some people accept new technology, others don't

ii) There are a number of idiomatic expressions involving tutto, one or two examples of which are given below:

Buon Natale a tutti quanti!   **sono contentissimi tutti e due**
Happy Christmas to all of you!   they are both very happy

iii) When the adjective certo precedes the noun it has the sense of 'some', 'some but not others', whereas after the noun it has the sense of 'sure' or 'indisputable':

certi voli sono stati rimandati a domani mattina
some flights have been postponed until tomorrow morning

certi si sono dichiarati contenti dei cambiamenti
certain people declared themselves happy with the changes

una certa signora Ferrari ha telefonato mezz'ora fa
a (certain) Signora Ferrari phoned half an hour ago

è una cosa certa! vincerà la nostra squadra
it's a sure thing, our team will win

DEMONSTRATIVE PRONOUNS AND ADJECTIVES

1 questo

questo/a/i/e (this, these) functions either as a pronoun or as an adjective. Note that as an adjective, the final -o or -a can be dropped before a noun beginning with a vowel (especially if it is the same vowel):

di chi è questo?
whose is this?

questi tulipani
these tulips

questa ragazza
this girl

questi sono i miei nipoti
these are my grandchildren

quest'aereo/questo aereo
this plane

2 quello

quello/a/i/e (that, those) functions both as a pronoun and as an adjective but the forms are slightly different in each case:

a) The pronoun forms are quello, quella, quelli and quelle:

avevo dimenticato il mio ombrello, così ho preso quello di mio padre
I had forgotten my umbrella so I took my father's

preferiscono quelli bianchi
they prefer those white ones

b) The adjectival forms resemble those of the definite article:

quel **libro**	that book	quei **libri**	those books
quell'**albergo**	that hotel	quegli **alberghi**	those hotels
quello **studente**	that student	quegli **studenti**	those students
quella **signora**	that lady	quelle **signore**	those ladies
quell'**agenzia**	that agency	quelle **agenzie**	those agencies

3 questo and quello

a) Proximity and distance may be emphasized by the addition after the pronoun of the appropriate adverbs of place, **qui** and **qua** (here) or **lì** and **là** (there):

ti piace questo qui? – no, preferisco quello lì
do you like this one here? – no, I prefer that one there

questa qua mi sembra un po' amara
I find this one here slightly bitter

b) As pronouns, **questo** and **quello** may be employed in the construction, 'the former ... the latter' (note, however, that **questo** means 'the latter' and **quello** means 'the former'):

ho visto il cliente francese e quello giapponese: questo vuole venire senz'altro, ma quello non si è ancora deciso
I've seen the French and Japanese customers: the latter definitely wants to come but the former hasn't decided yet

> ## Note
>
> - The latter (**questo/a/i/e**) is always mentioned first.
> - One may use **il primo ... il secondo** or, more commonly, **il primo ... l'ultimo** instead of **questo ... quello**:
>   **Totti e Rooney sono capicannonieri: il primo è italiano, il secondo inglese**
>   Totti and Rooney are leading goal scorers: the first is Italian and the second English
> - There is also an older invariable form **questi ... quegli** (the former ... the latter) which will be found in literary language.

4 costui and colui

Two other sets of demonstrative pronouns should be mentioned although their use is declining:

costui	this man	costei	this woman	costoro	these people
colui	that man	colei	that woman	coloro	those people

coloro che non vogliono entrare rimangano fuori
those who don't want to come in should stay outside

These pronouns often have a derogatory meaning:

chi è costui?
who (on earth) is that guy?

5 ciò

ciò (that) is an invariable neuter pronoun referring to objects or ideas mentioned previously:

ciò non è vero   **e con ciò?**
that's not true   so what?

tutto ciò mi sorprende veramente
that all really surprises me

6 stesso and medesimo

stesso and medesimo mean 'same' and agree with their subject (the former is more common in the spoken language):

frequentiamo lo stesso circolo sportivo
we go to the same sports club

stesso, however, can also be used as a reinforcing word, in which case it always follows the noun or pronoun:

il direttore stesso non sa che fare
the director himself doesn't know what to do

è partita la sera stessa   **l'ho vista io stesso**
she left that very evening   I saw her myself

Note that the third person singular and plural reflexive pronoun **sé** drops the acute accent when followed by **stesso**:

ama solo se stesso
he loves only himself

 J RELATIVE PRONOUNS

1 che

a) **che** means 'who', 'whom', 'which' and 'that' and is invariable. It refers to both people and things. It may be used only with the function of a subject or of a direct object pronoun:

il ragazzo che ha gridato
the boy who shouted

sono persone che conosco da parecchi anni
they are people whom I've known for several years

questo è il romanzo che ha vinto il premio Strega
this is the novel that/which won the Strega prize

> *Note*
>
> The relative pronoun may not be omitted in Italian as it often is in English:
>
> **la lavastoviglie che ho comprato l'anno scorso**
> the dishwasher I bought last year
> **la ragazza che ho visto**
> the girl I saw

For the agreement of the past participle after a relative pronoun see p 174.

b) **il che**

   che is occasionally preceded by the article **il**, thus acquiring the sense 'something which':

   è stata molto ammalata, il che mi è dispiaciuto molto
   she was very ill, which upset me

   ha chiesto di mia madre, del che ero molto grato
   he/she asked after my mother, for which I was very grateful

c) **quel che, quello che** and **ciò che**

   quel che, quello che and **ciò che** are all relative pronouns meaning 'what'. They refer to things, not persons, and are interchangeable:

   raccontami quel che/ciò che hai fatto
   tell me what you've been doing

   mangio ciò che voglio
   I eat what I like

   non riusciamo a sentire quello che dici
   we can't hear what you're saying

   'All that' is translated by **tutto quel/quello, ciò che**. English is very apt to miss out the relative pronoun in a way that is impossible in Italian:

   ecco tutto quel che posso dirle
   that's all I can tell you/her

2 cui as a pronoun

a) Since the relative pronoun **che** may be used only as a subject or a direct object pronoun, with a preposition it is necessary to substitute the invariable pronoun **cui**:

   il pianista di cui ti ho parlato tanto
   the pianist I have so often told you about

   la signora con cui sono andata al concerto
   the lady with whom I went to the concert

   la ragione per cui ho rifiutato è questa
   the reason I refused is this

b) The preposition a before cui meaning 'to which', 'to whom' can
be omitted:

questo è il progetto (a) cui ho preso parte
this is the project I took part in

3 cui as a possessive

cui meaning 'whose', 'of whom' or 'of which' is invariable. It is
positioned between the definite article and the noun:

questa è la signora il cui figlio è gravemente malato
this is the lady whose son is seriously ill

è un paese i cui costumi mi sono totalmente sconosciuti
it is a country whose customs (the customs of which) are totally
  unknown to me

qui ci sono ville i cui proprietari abitano all'estero
here there are villas whose owners live abroad

4 il quale

The pronouns cui and che may be substituted by il quale (la quale/
i quali/le quali). These pronouns refer both to people and things and
agree in number and gender with the subject.

a) As a substitute for che, il quale is usually employed only in order
to avoid ambiguity:

**la moglie del signor Galli, la quale ha organizzato quella gita a
  San Gimignano**
Signor Galli's wife, who organized that trip to San Gimignano

b) When substituted for cui preceded by a preposition, the examples
given in section 2 above would become:

il pianista del quale ti ho parlato tanto
the pianist I have so often told you about

la signora con la quale sono andata al concerto
the lady with whom I went to the concert

la ragione per la quale ho rifiutato è questa
the reason I refused is this

c) When substituted for cui in its possessive function, the examples given in section 3 above would become:

questa è la signora il figlio della quale è gravemente malato
this is the lady whose son is seriously ill

è un paese i costumi del quale mi sono totalmente sconosciuti
it is a country whose customs are totally unknown to me

qui ci sono ville i proprietari delle quali abitano all' estero
here there are villas whose owners live abroad

5 chi

chi is an invariable pronoun which has two meanings: 'the one/ones who' and 'anyone who'. It refers only to people and must be followed by a singular verb. It is commonly used in proverbs:

chi vivrà, vedrà   **ride bene chi ride ultimo**
only time will tell   he who laughs last laughs longest

chi vuole andare al mare con questo freddo è pazzo
anyone who wants to go to the seaside in this cold is mad

K INTERROGATIVE AND EXCLAMATORY PRONOUNS AND ADJECTIVES

Interrogative pronouns and adjectives are used in direct and indirect questions. Some words can function both as pronouns and as adjectives:

1 Interrogative pronouns

a) chi (who) is an invariable interrogative pronoun which refers only to people:

chi ve l'ha detto?   **con chi hai cenato?**
who told you?   who did you have dinner with?

di chi è questa bici?   dimmi chi sei
whose bike is this?   tell me who you are

b) che, che cosa, cosa (what) are invariable interrogative pronouns
   which refer only to things:

che hai detto?   che cosa c'è da vedere?
what did you say?   what is there to see?

cosa stai facendo?   ditemi che cosa avete visto
what are you doing?   tell me what you saw

Note, however, that the use of cosa without che would be less
appropriate in a more formal context.

c) quale/i (which (one/ones)) is an interrogative pronoun which
   refers both to people and to things:

quale preferisce, signora?   qual è il vostro cantante preferito?
which one do you prefer, Madam?   who is your favourite singer?

qual è la tua camera?   quali vuoi buttar via?
which is your bedroom?   which ones do you want to throw
                                        out?

mi ha chiesto qual era il significato di questo
he asked me what the meaning of this was

d) quanto/a/i/e (how much/many):

quanto hai pagato quelle scarpe?
how much did you pay for those shoes?

mi dica quanto le devo, signore
tell me how much I owe you, sir

quante ne hai incontrato/e?
how many of them did you meet?

2 Interrogative adjectives

a) che (what) is invariable:

che tipo di vacanze ti piace di più?
what sort of holiday do you like best?

che programma vuoi guardare?
what programme do you want to watch?

b) quale/i (what), (which (one/ones)):

per quale motivo hai convocato questa riunione?
for what reason did you call this meeting?

quale camicetta ti metti stamattina?
which blouse are you putting on this morning?

quali alberghi ci sono nei dintorni?
what hotels are there round here?

c) quanto/a/i/e (how much/many):

quante università ci sono adesso in Italia?
how many universities are there now in Italy?

quanta disoccupazione c'è attualmente in Gran Bretagna?
what is the current level of unemployment in Great Britain?

3 Exclamatory uses of che, come and quanto

che bello!	**che noia!**	**che puzza!**
how lovely!	how boring!	what a stink!
che brutta giornata!	**che fame!**	
what a horrible day!	I'm so hungry!	
come sei gentile!	**come sei permaloso!**	
how nice of you!	how touchy you are!	
quanta gente!	**quante storie!**	
what a crowd!	what a lot of nonsense!	

6 VERBS

A REGULAR CONJUGATIONS

1 Conjugations

There are three conjugations in Italian, which are determined by the infinitive endings. The first conjugation verbs, the largest category, end in -are (eg parlare) and will be referred to as -are verbs; the second conjugation verbs end in -ere (eg credere) and will be referred to as -ere verbs; the third conjugation verbs, the smallest category, end in -ire (eg sentire) and will be referred to as -ire verbs.

2 Simple tenses

The simple tenses in Italian are:

- ❏ present
- ❏ imperfect
- ❏ future
- ❏ conditional
- ❏ past historic
- ❏ present subjunctive
- ❏ imperfect subjunctive

For the uses of the different tenses, see **pp 136-144.**

3 Formation of tenses

The tenses are formed by adding the following endings to the stem of the infinitive as set out in the following section:

a) *PRESENT*: stem of the infinitive + the following endings:

-ARE *verbs*	-ERE *verbs*
-o, -i, -a	-o, -i, -e
-iamo, -ate, -ano	-iamo, -ete, -ono

PARLARE	CREDERE
parlo	credo
parli	credi
parla	crede
parliamo	crediamo
parlate	credete
parlano	credono

Note that verbs ending in -ere can have a stressed ending (eg vedere) or an unstressed ending (eg credere). Their conjugation remains the same.

```
-IRE verbs
-o, -i, -e,                          -isco, -isci, -isce
-iamo, -ite, -ono                    -iamo, -ite, -iscono

SENTIRE                              CAPIRE
sento                                capisco
senti                                capisci
sente                                capisce
sentiamo                             capiamo
sentite                              capite
sentono                              capiscono
```

As seen above, many verbs of the third conjugation insert -isc- between the stem and the ending in the singular and in the third person plural of the present indicative and subjunctive. The most common ones are: capire (to understand), costruire (to build), finire (to finish), preferire (to prefer), pulire (to clean).

Note that the stress of the third person plural of the three conjugations always falls on the root of the verb and *never* on the ending, eg: capiscono

b) *IMPERFECT*: stem of the infinitive + the following endings:

-ARE *verbs*	-ERE *verbs*	-IRE *verbs*
-avo, -avi, -ava	-evo, -evi, -eva	-ivo, -ivi, -iva
-avamo, -avate,	-evamo, -evate,	-ivamo, -ivate,
-avano	-evano	-ivano
parlavo	credevo	sentivo
parllavi	credevi	sentivi
parlava	credeva	sentiva
parlavamo	credevamo	sentivamo
parlavate	credevate	sentivate
parlavano	credevano	sentivano

c) *FUTURE*: infinitive removing the final -e + the following endings:

-ò, -ai, -à, -emo, -ete, -anno

Note that regular verbs ending in -are change the characteristic vowel a into e:

parlerò	crederò	sentirò
parlerai	crederai	sentirai
parlerà	crederà	sentirà
parleremo	crederemo	sentiremo
parlerete	crederete	sentirete
parleranno	crederanno	sentiranno

d) *CONDITIONAL*: stem of the future + the following endings:

-ei, -esti, -ebbe, -emmo, -este, -ebbero

parlerei	crederei	sentirei
parleresti	crederesti	sentiresti
parlerebbe	crederebbe	sentirebbe
parleremmo	crederemmo	sentiremmo
parlereste	credereste	sentireste
parlerebbero	crederebbero	sentirebbero

e) *PAST HISTORIC*: stem of the infinitive + the following endings:

-ARE verbs	-ERE verbs	-IRE verbs
-ai, -asti, -ò	-ei, -esti, -é	-ii, -isti, -ì
-ammo, -aste,	-emmo, -este,	-immo, -iste, -irono
-arono	-erono	
parlai	credei	sentii
parlasti	credesti	sentisti
parlò	credé	sentì
parlammo	credemmo	sentimmo
parlaste	credeste	sentiste
parlarono	crederono	sentirono

Note that most verbs ending in -ere (but not those whose root ends in t, like potere) have alternative forms for the first person singular and the third person singular and plural: -etti,-ette, -ettero (eg credetti, credette, credettero). These forms are used just as frequently.

f) *PRESENT SUBJUNCTIVE*: stem of the infinitive + the following endings:

-ARE *verbs*	-ERE *verbs*	-IRE *verbs*
-i, -i, -i,	-a, -a, -a,	-a, -a, -a,
-iamo, -iate, -ino	-iamo, -iate, -ano	-iamo, -iate, -ano
parli	creda	senta
parli	creda	senta
parli	creda	senta
parliamo	crediamo	sentiamo
parliate	crediate	sentiate
parlino	credano	sentano

g) *IMPERFECT SUBJUNCTIVE*: stem of the infinitive + the
   following endings:

-ARE *verbs*	-ERE *verbs*	-IRE *verbs*
-assi, -assi, -asse,	-essi, -essi, -esse,	-issi, -issi, -isse,
-assimo, -aste,	-essimo, -este,	-issimo, -iste,
-assero	-essero	-issero
parlassi	credessi	sentissi
parlassi	credessi	sentissi
parlasse	credesse	sentisse
parlassimo	credessimo	sentissimo
parlaste	credeste	sentiste
parlassero	credessero	sentissero

For the conjugation of the auxiliary verbs essere *(to be) and* avere
(to have) and of the main irregular verbs, see pp 185–205.

B STANDARD SPELLING IRREGULARITIES

In some first conjugation verbs, spelling changes occur to
ensure that the pronunciation remains the same throughout the
conjugation:

1 First conjugation verbs ending in -care and -gare

Verbs ending in -care and -gare retain the same sound which the
c and g have in the infinitive by inserting an h before i and e:

CERCARE		PAGARE	
cerco	cercherò	pago	pagherò
cerchi	cercherai	paghi	pagherai
cerca	cercherà	paga	pagherà
cerchiamo	cercheremo	paghiamo	pagheremo
cercate	cercherete	pagate	pagherete
cercano	cercheranno	pagano	pagheranno

2 Verbs ending in -ciare, -giare and -sciare

Verbs ending in -ciare, -giare and -sciare drop the i of the stem whenever it precedes i and e:

COMINCIARE		MANGIARE	
comincio	comincerò	mangio	mangerò
cominci	comincerai	mangi	mangerai
comincia	comincerà	mangia	mangerà
cominciamo	cominceremo	mangiamo	mangeremo
cominciate	comincerete	mangiate	mangerete
cominciano	cominceranno	mangiano	mangeranno

LASCIARE	
lascio	lascerò
lasci	lascerai
lascia	lascerà
lasciamo	lasceremo
lasciate	lascerete
lasciano	lasceranno

3 Verbs ending in -gnare

Verbs ending in -gnare keep the i when it is part of the ending, ie in the first person plural of the present indicative and in the first and second persons plural of the present subjunctive:

BAGNARE
bagniamo   **bagnate** *(present indicative)*
bagniamo   **bagniate** *(present subjunctive)*

4. Verbs ending in -gliare

Verbs ending in -gliare keep the i before o, a and e but drop it before another i:

SBADIGLIARE
sbadiglio
sbadiglia
sbadiglierei *(conditional)*
sbadigli *(present subjunctive)*

5 Verbs ending in -iare

Verbs ending in -iare in which the i of the stem is stressed retain this i in the second person singular of the present indicative, but they lose it otherwise:

SCIARE	**CAMBIARE**
scio (stressed)	cambio (unstressed)
scii	cambi
scia	cambia
sciamo	cambiamo
sciate	cambiate
sciano	cambiano

6 Second conjugation verbs ending in -cere, -gere and -scere

Verbs ending in -cere, -gere and -scere change the pronunciation of the last consonant of the stem according to the first vowel of the ending:

VINCERE	**LEGGERE**	**CONOSCERE**
vinco	leggo	conosco
vinci	leggi	conosci
vince	legge	conosce
vinciamo	leggiamo	conosciamo
vincete	leggete	conoscete
vincono	leggono	conoscono

The verb fuggire (to escape) also behaves in the same way: fuggo, fuggi, fugge, fuggiamo, fuggite, fuggono

Note that the verbs cuocere (to cook) and cucire (to sew) retain the 'soft' sound of the infinitive throughout:

cuocio, cuoci, cuoce, cuociamo, cuocete, cuociono
cucio, cuci, cuce, cuciamo, cucite, cuciono

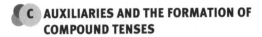

C AUXILIARIES AND THE FORMATION OF COMPOUND TENSES

1 Formation

a) The two auxiliary verbs **avere** and **essere** are used with the past participle of a verb to form compound tenses.

b) *The past participle*

The regular past participle is formed by taking the stem of the infinitive and adding the following endings:

-ARE *verbs*	-ERE *verbs*	-IRE *verbs*
parl(are) + ato	cred(ere) + uto	sent(ire) + ito
parlato	creduto	sentito

For the agreement of past participles see pp 174-5.

c) *Compound tenses*

In Italian there are seven compound tenses: perfect, pluperfect, future perfect, past conditional (perfect conditional), past anterior, perfect subjunctive and pluperfect subjunctive.

3 Verbs conjugated with AVERE

PERFECT	PLUPERFECT
present of **avere** + past participle	imperfect of **avere** + past participle
ho parlato	avevo parlato
hai parlato	avevi parlato
ha parlato	aveva parlato
abbiamo parlato	avevamo parlato
avete parlato	avevate parlato
hanno parlato	avevano parlato

FUTURE PERFECT	PAST CONDITIONAL
future of **avere** + past participle	conditional of **avere** + past participle
avrò parlato	avrei parlato
avrai parlato	avresti parlato
avrà parlato	avrebbe parlato
avremo parlato	avremmo parlato
avrete parlato	avreste parlato
avranno parlato	avrebbero parlato

PAST ANTERIOR	
past historic of **avere** + past participle	
ebbi parlato	
avesti parlato	
ebbe parlato	
avemmo parlato	
aveste parlato	
ebbero parlato	

PERFECT SUBJUNCTIVE	PLUPERFECT SUBJUNCTIVE
present subjunctive of **avere** + past participle	imperfect subjunctive of **avere** + past participle
abbia parlato	avessi parlato
abbia parlato	avessi parlato
abbia parlato	avesse parlato
abbiamo parlato	avessimo parlato
abbiate parlato	aveste parlato
abbiano parlato	avessero parlato

3 Verbs conjugated with ESSERE

PERFECT	PLUPERFECT
present of **essere** + past participle	imperfect of **essere** + past participle
sono arrivato/a	ero arrivato/a
sei arrivato/a	eri arrivato/a
è arrivato/a	era arrivato/a
siamo arrivati/e	eravamo arrivati/e
siete arrivati/e	eravate arrivati/e
sono arrivati/e	erano arrivati/e

FUTURE PERFECT	PAST CONDITIONAL
future of **essere** + past participle	conditional of **essere** + past participle
sarò arrivato/a	sarei arrivato/a
sarai arrivato/a	saresti arrivato/a
sarà arrivato/a	sarebbe arrivato/a
saremo arrivati/e	saremmo arrivati/e
sarete arrivati/e	sareste arrivati/e
saranno arrivati/e	sarebbero arrivati/e

PAST ANTERIOR	
past historic of **essere** + past participle	
fui arrivato/a	
fosti arrivato/a	
fu arrivato/a	
fummo arrivati/e	
foste arrivati/e	
furono arrivati/e	

PERFECT SUBJUNCTIVE	PLUPERFECT SUBJUNCTIVE
present subjunctive of **essere** + past participle	imperfect subjunctive of **essere** + past participle
sia arrivato/a	fossi arrivato/a
sia arrivato/a	fossi arrivato/a
sia arrivato/a	fosse arrivato/a
siamo arrivati/e	fossimo arrivati/e
siate arrivati/e	foste arrivati/e
siano arrivati/e	fossero arrivati/e

4 AVERE or ESSERE?

a) *Verbs conjugated with* avere

The compound tenses of most verbs (and all transitive verbs) are formed with avere:

ho parlato italiano tutto il giorno
I spoke Italian all day

Pietro ha fumato per dieci anni e poi ha smesso
Pietro smoked for ten years and then he stopped

b) *Verbs conjugated with* essere

   i) all reflexive verbs (*see* p 127):

     mi sono divertito molto
     I enjoyed myself very much

   ii) some verbs that indicate movement or staying in one place:

andare	to go
arrivare	to arrive
cadere	to fall
emigrare	to emigrate
entrare	to enter
fuggire	to escape
partire	to leave
passare	to go through, to drop in
restare	to stay
rimanere	to remain
sorgere	to rise
tornare	to return
uscire	to go out
venire	to come

era emigrato negli anni sessanta ma ora è tornato
he emigrated in the sixties but now he is back

non è ancora passato a salutarci
he hasn't yet dropped in to say hello

è rimasta solo dieci minuti e poi è uscita
she stayed only ten minutes and then she went out

iii) verbs which indicate changes of psychological or physical processes linked with the subject:

apparire/comparire	to appear
arrossire	to blush
dimagrire	to lose weight
divenire/diventare	to become
essere	to be
impallidire	to turn pale
impazzire	to go mad
ingrassare	to put on weight
marcire	to rot
morire	to die
nascere	to be born
parere/sembrare	to seem
scomparire	to disappear
scoppiare	to blow up

è ingrassato molto da quando è andato in pensione
he has put on a lot of weight since he retired

non mi è sembrato giusto dirglielo
it did not seem right to tell him about it

Note how English and Italian differ in their use of tenses with nascere (to be born):

sono nato nel 1970
I was born in 1970

iv) the verb piacere and the following verbs, which are similar to piacere in their construction:

bastare	to be sufficient
dispiacere	to be sorry
importare	to matter
mancare	to lack, to miss
occorrere/servire	to be necessary

Note that the construction of these verbs in Italian is different from English: they take an indirect object followed by the verb and the subject:

non mi è mai piaciuto il suo atteggiamento
I never liked his/her/your attitude

non gli è mai mancato il coraggio **le è bastato uno sguardo**
he never lacked courage   one look was enough for her

v) impersonal verbs:

accadere
capitare   to happen
succedere

mi è capitato spesso di incontrarlo ai giardini
I often happened to come across him in the park

Impersonal verbs referring to the weather can take either auxiliary:

è/ha piovuto   era/aveva nevicato
it has rained   it had snowed

vi) other verbs:

costare	to cost
dipendere	to depend
esistere	to exist
intervenire	to intervene
prevalere	to prevail
ricorrere a	to turn to
risultare	to result
riuscire	to succeed
valere	to be worth
volerci	to take, to require

il nuovo telefonino gli è costato un occhio della testa
his new mobile cost him an arm and a leg

non erano affatto intervenuti nella faccenda
they had not intervened at all in the matter

sono ricorso al loro aiuto più volte
I have turned to them many times for help

ci è voluta tutta la mia pazienza per convincerla
it took all my patience to convince her

c) *Verbs which can take either* essere *or* avere

Some verbs take avere when they have an object, essere when they do not. Here are some of the most common ones:

aumentare	to increase
cessare/smettere	to stop
cominciare	to start
continuare	to continue
diminuire	to diminish
finire	to finish
guarire	to cure, recover
migliorare	to improve
salire	to go up
scendere	to go down
seguire	to follow
servire	to serve, to be necessary
vivere	to live

il pilota ha aumentato la velocità
the pilot increased speed

recentemente i prezzi sono aumentati
prices have gone up recently

ho cambiato la macchina l'anno scorso
I changed my car last year

tutti i numeri telefonici di Londra sono cambiati
all London telephone numbers have changed

hanno migliorato la qualità dei lettori DVD
they have improved the quality of DVD players

la mia salute è migliorata con la ginnastica
my health has improved with exercise

> ## Note
>
> Some of these verbs can take a preposition + infinitive; in this case their auxiliary is always avere:
>
> **ho cominciato a studiare due ore fa**
> I started studying two hours ago
>
> **hanno finito di riparare la lavatrice?**
> have they finished repairing the washing machine?

d) *Verbs which have a different meaning according to the auxiliary*

convenire	to agree/to gather
correre	to run/to run somewhere
mancare	to lack, to neglect/to be lacking, to be missing

i sindacati hanno convenuto che lo sciopero era necessario
the trade unions have agreed that the strike was necessary

i partecipanti erano convenuti da ogni parte d'Italia
the participants had gathered from every part of Italy

in quell'occasione hai mancato di tatto
on that occasion you lacked tact

sei mancato agli appuntamenti troppe volte
you have missed your appointments too often

> ## Note
>
> • correre, saltare and volare usually take avere, but take essere when followed by a specification of place:
>
> **ha corso finché non gli è mancato il fiato**
> he ran until he was out of breath
>
> **è corso alla stazione ma non è arrivato in tempo**
> he ran to the station but he didn't make it in time

Note—cont'd

- volare also takes essere when its subject indicates a length of time:

  le ferie quest'anno sono volate!
  the holidays really flew by this year!

  il tempo era proprio volato
  time had really flown

e) *Verbs which can take either auxiliary, with no change in meaning*

appartenere	to belong
giovare	to be useful, to be good
vivere	to live

ha/è appartenuto a quell'associazione per anni
he belonged to that society for years

le ha giovato/le è giovata molto l'aria di mare
the sea air was very good for her

hai/sei vissuto in questa casa per troppo tempo
you have lived in this house too long

Note

Modal verbs (ie dovere, potere and volere) accompanying an infinitive requiring essere normally take essere too, but the form with avere is also used:

non è potuta/ha potuto andare alla riunione
she could not go to the meeting

non sono potuto/ho potuto rimanere perché non avevo più soldi
I could not stay because I had no money left

D REFLEXIVE VERBS

1 Definition

Reflexive verbs are so called because they 'reflect' the action back onto the subject. Reflexive verbs are always accompanied by a reflexive pronoun, for example in the sentence 'I washed myself with soap', "myself" is a reflexive pronoun.

lavo la macchina ogni settimana　　**mi lavo**
I wash the car every week　　　　　　I wash myself

2 Reflexive pronouns

They are:

PERSON	SINGULAR	PLURAL
1st	mi	ci
	myself	ourselves
2nd	ti	vi
	yourself	yourselves
3rd	si	si
	himself, herself, itself, oneself, yourself *(polite)*	themselves, yourselves *(polite)*

Note that Italian reflexive pronouns are often not translated in English:

mi chiedo se ...　　　　　**si prendono gioco di me**
I wonder if ...　　　　　　　they're making fun of me

Note also that in dictionaries, you will find reflexive verbs in the infinitive with the reflexive pronoun **si** replacing the final **e**:

lavare　　　　　　**lavarsi**
to wash　　　　　　to wash oneself

difendere　　　　**difendersi**
to defend　　　　　to defend oneself

3 Conjugation of reflexive verbs

a) *Simple tenses*

These are formed in the same way as for non-reflexive verbs, except that a reflexive pronoun is used.

b) *Compound tenses*

These are formed with the auxiliary essere followed by the past participle of the verb.

A full conjugation table is given on **p 197**. *For agreement of reflexive verbs see* **p 175**.

4 Position of reflexive pronouns

The position of reflexive pronouns is the same as for all other unstressed personal pronouns: they always precede the verb except in the second persons of the imperative and in the non-finite forms of the verb (eg infinitive, gerund and participle). In the negative form of the second person singular and plural of the imperative the pronoun can either precede or follow the verb:

vestiti!
get dressed!

non vestirti!/non ti vestire!
don't get dressed!

la sposa si è vestita da sola
the bride got dressed without help

voleva vestirsi da sola
she wanted to get dressed on her own

vestitasi, andò in chiesa
having got dressed, she left for church

vestendosi si guardava allo specchio
while getting dressed he/she looked at himself/herself in the mirror

5 Types of reflexive verbs

a) Verbs in which the action reflects back onto the subject, equivalent to English reflexive constructions with '-self':

ti lavi
you wash yourself

si è ucciso
he killed himself

vi servite
you help yourselves

b) Verbs which are followed by a direct object; in this case the reflexive pronoun has the function of an indirect object (eg it means 'to/for me, to/for you', *etc*):

mi sono comprata un nuovo cellulare
I bought myself a new mobile

ci siamo preparate la cena in mezz'ora
we prepared the dinner (for ourselves) in half an hour

c) Many transitive verbs can be used reflexively to indicate a reciprocal action, usually translated in English with 'each other' or 'one another':

amarsi	to love	
baciarsi	to kiss	
conoscersi	to know	each other/one another
odiarsi	to hate	
scriversi	to write to	

si conoscono da quando erano bambini
they have known each other since they were children

si scrivono regolarmente
they write to each other regularly

d) Verbs which indicate movement of the body, which in English would be translated by an intransitive verb followed by an adverb, eg 'to lean over', 'to climb up' *etc*:

alzarsi	to get up
affacciarsi	to lean out

arrampicarsi	to climb up
chinarsi	to lean down
coricarsi	to lie down
muoversi	to move
sedersi	to sit down
spostarsi	to move

Note that some of these verbs can also have the normal transitive function:

ho alzato il vaso per vedere cosa c'era sotto
I lifted the vase to see what was underneath

ho mosso la pedina troppo presto
I moved my pawn too soon

e) Verbs which denote physiological or psychological processes, often translated in English with 'to get' or 'to become' followed by an adjective:

addormentarsi	to fall asleep
affezionarsi a	to become fond of
ammalarsi	to become ill
annoiarsi	to get bored
arrabbiarsi	to get angry
confondersi	to get mixed up
divertirsi	to enjoy oneself
offendersi	to get offended
pentirsi di	to regret
svegliarsi	to wake up
vergognarsi	to be ashamed

si affezionò molto a quel cane
he/she became very fond of that dog

mi sono annoiata mortalmente a quella festa
I got terribly bored at that party

non ti vergogni di quello che hai fatto?
are you not ashamed of what you have done?

Note that some of these verbs can have a normal transitive function:

ho addormentato mio figlio con una ninna-nanna
I sang my son to sleep with a lullaby

ha confuso la madre con la figlia
he/she mistook the mother for the daughter

Note, however, the alternative transitive and reflexive forms of the verbs dimenticare and ricordare:

ricordo molto bene quella ragazza
I remember that girl very well

mi ricordo molto bene di quella ragazza
I remember that girl very well

dimentico sempre quello che devo comprare
I always forget what I have to buy

mi dimentico sempre di quello che devo comprare
I always forget what I have to buy

f) Verbs which are used in the reflexive form as an alternative to their normal transitive form, normally in colloquial Italian, without any substantial difference in their meaning:

ci siamo mangiati un bel piatto di pastasciutta
we had a nice plate of pasta

non me lo sogno nemmeno!
I wouldn't dream of it!

appena alzata mi bevo una tazza di caffè
as soon as I get up I drink a cup of coffee

E IMPERSONAL VERBS

Impersonal verbs in English are always in the third person singular and take 'it' for their subject. In Italian they are more complicated than in English and can be grouped in the following way:

1 Verbs and phrases describing the weather:

a) fare + adjective:

fa bello/caldo
it's fine/warm

fa fresco/freddo
it's cool/cold

domani farà bello
the weather will be good tomorrow

fa molto freddo
it's very cold

b) fare + noun:

fa bel tempo
the weather is nice

fa brutto tempo
the weather is bad

One can also use il tempo è bello/brutto in place of these impersonal expressions.
Note also the expressions:

fa giorno
it's daylight

fa notte
it's dark

c) Other impersonal verbs and verbs used impersonally to describe the weather:

gelare: **gela**	it's freezing
grandinare: **grandina**	it's hailing
nevicare: **nevica**	it's snowing
piovere: **piove**	it's raining
tuonare: **tuona**	it's thundering
tirare vento: **tira vento**	it's windy

Note that some of these can be used personally:

sto gelando
I am freezing

2 Impersonal expressions formed with **essere** followed by an adjective:

è difficile it's difficult	**è facile** it's easy	**è necessario** it's necessary
è inutile it's useless	**è possibile** it's possible	**è sufficiente** it's sufficient

è difficile parlarne
it's difficult to talk about it

è necessario che tu sia presente
you have to be present

For the use of the subjunctive see pp 147-8.

3 Verbs expressing pleasure, displeasure, need, lack *etc* are followed by a dependent clause whose verb can be a subjunctive or an infinitive, depending on whether the subject of the second verb is mentioned (*see* rules of the subjunctive, pp 146-8):

a) piacere *(to like)*, dispiacere/rincrescere *(to regret, to be sorry)*

non mi piace che frequenti quel ragazzo
I don't like you going out with that boy

mi è rincresciuto molto dover rinunciare alla festa
I was very sorry to have to miss the party

Note that these verbs can have a personal construction when accompanied by a noun which is their subject:

vi piacciono le macchine sportive?
do you like sports cars?

l'ultimo modello della Fiat non mi dispiace affatto
I quite like the latest Fiat model

tu piaci molto al professore
the teacher likes you a lot

b) accadere, avvenire, succedere *(to happen)*

accadeva spesso che la incontrasse in centro
he/she often met her in town

ogni tanto succede che la mia stampante si fermi
my printer sometimes just stops

è accaduta una disgrazia   **che cosa è successo?**
there has been an accident   what happened?

c) bastare *(to be enough)*, restare *(to be left, to remain)*, mancare *(to be missing/lacking)*, servire/occorrere *(to be necessary)*

basta seguire le istruzioni   **non mi resta che piangere**
just follow the instructions   all I can do now is cry

manca solo che ti dimentichi di venire!
all we need now is for you to forget to come!

occorre sbrinare il frigo ogni tanto
you have to defrost the fridge every now and then

queste sedie non basteranno per tutti
these chairs won't be enough for everybody

che cosa manca per la cena di domani?
what do we need for tomorrow's dinner?

d) parere/sembrare *(to seem)*

pare che vada a trovare i figli ogni week-end
it seems that he/she goes to see his/her children every weekend

mi sembrava strano che non avesse capito
I thought it was curious that he/she hadn't understood

dopo l'incidente pare/sembra invecchiato di dieci anni
he looks ten years older since his accident

4 Other common impersonal verbs:

a) trattarsi di *(to be a matter of)*

This may be followed by a noun, a pronoun or an infinitive:

si tratta del tuo avvenire
it's about your future

di che cosa si tratta?
what is it about?

si tratta di scoprire chi l'ha fatto
we must find who did it

b) bisognare *(to be necessary)*

bisogna che tu parta immediatamente
you must leave immediately

non bisogna perdere la calma
one must keep calm

> ## Note
>
> The verb **bisognare** is only used in the third person singular as an impersonal verb; the transitive verb 'to need' translates as **avere bisogno di**:
>
> **ho bisogno di un nuovo paio di occhiali da sole**
> I need a new pair of sunglasses
>
> **non ha mai bisogno di aiuto**
> he/she never needs help

c) volerci *(to be necessary)*

Note that **volerci** must be used in the third person plural when it refers to a plural:

ci vuole molta pazienza per sopportarti!
it takes a lot of patience to put up with you!

per andare da Genova a Milano ci vogliono due ore di macchina
it takes two hours by car to go from Genoa to Milan

F USE OF TENSES

For the formation of the various tenses see pp 111–15 *and* 118–26.

1 Present

The present is used to describe what someone does or is doing or something that happens regularly or that is happening at the time of speaking.

a) *Present states*

sto bene
I'm well

b) *Regular actions*

lavora in fabbrica
he/she works in a factory

vado raramente al cinema
I seldom go to the cinema

c) *Actions which take place at the time of speaking*

dove vai? – vado di sopra
where are you going? – I'm going upstairs

che cosa fai? – controllo il motore
what are you doing? – I'm checking the engine

> ### Note
>
> • stare + *gerund* corresponds to the English present progressive 'to be ... -ing':
>
> **sto leggendo l'ultimo libro di Moravia**
> I'm reading Moravia's last book
>
> • stare + per + *infinitive* corresponds to the English 'to be about to ...':
>
> **l'aereo sta per atterrare**
> the plane is about to land

d) *General truths and proverbs*

l'ore è un metallo prezioso
gold is a precious metal

non è tutto oro quel che luccica
all that glitters is not gold

e) *Imminent or programmed future actions*

domani c'è un programma interessante alla TV
there's an interesting programme on TV tomorrow

fra un anno mi sposo
I'm getting married in a year

esco fra un'ora
I'm going out in an hour

torno subito
I'll be right back

f) The present tense can be used in written Italian as an alternative to the past historic to indicate past actions referring to historical or literary events, giving them a more immediate and lively tone:

il 25 aprile 1945 gli Alleati liberano Milano e Genova
on 25 April 1945 the Allies liberated Milan and Genoa

la scoperta dell'America segna l'inizio dell'età moderna
the discovery of America marks the beginning of the modern age

g) The present tense is used to render the English present perfect when an action which started in the past is still continuing (*see also* pp 139-41):

studio l'inglese da due anni
I have been studying English for two years

non fuma da più di un mese
he/she hasn't smoked for more than a month

2 Imperfect

The imperfect is a past tense used to express what someone was doing or what someone used to do or to describe something in the past. The imperfect refers particularly to something that *continued* over a period of time, as opposed to something that happened at a specific point in time.

a) *Continuous actions*

The imperfect describes an action that was happening when something else took place:

leggeva il giornale quando è suonato il campanello
he/she was reading the newspaper when the doorbell rang

b) *Repeated or regular actions in the past*

la incontravo spesso in Via Roma
I often met her in Via Roma

quando lavoravo in quella ditta mi stancavo molto
I used to get very tired when I worked for that company

c) *Descriptions in the past*

c'era una bella vista sul mare
there was a beautiful view of the sea

l'acqua di quel lago era sempre limpida
the water in the lake was always clear

il tempo era brutto quel giorno
the weather was bad that day

aveva i capelli biondi e gli occhi azzurri
he/she had fair hair and blue eyes

Note

• stare + *gerund* corresponds to the English past progressive 'to be ...-ing':

stava guardando il suo programma preferito
he/she was watching his/her favourite programme

> *Note—cont'd*
>
> • stare + per + *infinitive* corresponds to the English 'to be about to ...':
>
> **stavamo per telefonarti quando sei arrivato**
> we were about to call you when you arrived
>
> • In colloquial Italian, the imperfect is sometimes used to replace the present or past conditional:
>
> **desidera, signora? – volevo del prosciutto**
> can I help you, madam? – I'd like some ham
>
> **dovevi dirmelo subito**
> you should have told me immediately
>
> **era meglio se me lo dicevi prima**
> it would have been better if you had told me before

d) The imperfect is also used to render the English pluperfect when an action which started in the past was still continuing at a given time (*see also* pp 140-1):

studiavo l'inglese da due anni
I had been studying English for two years

non fumava da più di un mese
he/she had not smoked for more than a month

3 Present perfect and past historic

(referred to as the PASSATO PROSSIMO *and the* PASSATO REMOTO *in the conjugation tables,* pp 187-205)

The use of the present perfect (passato prossimo) and the past historic (passato remoto) varies geographically in Italy.

a) In the more central parts of Italy a distinction is made between the two. The present perfect is used to refer to a past action which is somehow related to the present. The past historic is used to refer to a completed action in the past:

present perfect:

l'ho visto ieri　　　　　　　　　**hai già mangiato?**
I saw him yesterday　　　　　　　have you eaten yet?

l'ho aspettato tutto il giorno
I've waited for him all day

past historic:

Dante nacque nel 1265
Dante was born in 1265

i Rossi rimasero in Germania per cinque anni
the Rossis remained in Germany for five years

The past historic is used as a narrative tense and is also a conversational tense in Italian.

b) In the North of Italy the present perfect is also used to refer to a completely past action, while in the south the past historic is sometimes used to refer to actions related to the present:

North　**te l'ho dato martedì**
South　**te lo diedi martedì**
　　　　I gave it to you on Tuesday
North　**ieri siamo andati al parco e ho perso il portafoglio**
South　**ieri andammo al parco e persi il portafoglio**
　　　　yesterday we went to the park and I lost my purse

4 Present perfect/past historic and imperfect compared

In English, the simple past ('did', 'went', 'prepared' *etc*) is used to describe both single and repeated actions in the past.

In Italian the present perfect/past historic describe *single* actions that happened (or started to happen) in a well defined space of time in the past:

l'Italia è diventata una repubblica nel 1947
Italy became a republic in 1947

sono stata a Venezia due anni fa
I went to Venice two years ago

i fuochi artificiali durarono dalle nove a mezzanotte
the fireworks lasted from nine o'clock till midnight

durante la siccità l'acqua venne razionata
during the drought water was rationed

Repeated, habitual or background actions, which are referred to
vaguely, with no clear restrictions on their duration and no mention
of their beginning and end are expressed by the *imperfect* (they
are sometimes signalled by 'used to' or 'I was ...-ing'). Thus 'I went'
should be translated 'andavo' or 'sono andato/andai' depending on
the nature of the action:

oggi la lezione di guida è durata due ore *(today only)*
present perfect
today the driving lesson lasted two hours

la lezione di guida durava un'ora *(normally)*
imperfect
the driving lesson lasted one hour

durante l'inverno è stato malato *(only that winter)*
present perfect
he was ill during the winter

durante l'inverno era sempre malato *(usually)*
imperfect
he was always ill during the winter

che cosa fece quando lo arrestarono?
past historic
what did he do when they arrested him?

che cosa faceva quando lo arrestarono?
imperfect
what was he doing when they arrested him?

5 Pluperfect

This compound tense is used to express what someone had done or had been doing, or something that had happened or had been happening. It can be used independently or in connection with a perfect or a past historic to express an action which happened previously:

non aveva mai fatto la permanente
she had never had her hair permed

gliel'avevo già detto migliaia di volte!
I had already told him a thousand times!

stava male perché aveva bevuto troppo
he/she wasn't well because he/she had drunk too much

non poté dirglielo perché era già partita
he/she couldn't tell her because she had already left

Note that adverbs like mai, già, prima, non ancora, dopo che, appena, quando, perché, siccome often accompany the pluperfect, stressing the fact that one action happened before the other.

6 Past anterior

This tense is used instead of the pluperfect to express an action that preceded another action in the past when the main verb is in the past historic. It is always introduced by dopo che (after), appena (as soon as) or quando (when):

dopo che furono entrati tutti, chiuse la porta
after everybody had come in, he/she closed the door

appena si furono sistemati, telefonarono a Claudio
as soon as they had got settled in, they rang Claudio

7 Future

a) This tense is used to express what someone will do or will be doing or something that will happen or will be happening:

il volo BA615 per Genova partirà con un'ora di ritardo
BA flight 615 to Genoa will leave one hour late

vi telefoneremo giovedì
we'll call you on Thursday

For the use of the present instead of the future, see p 137.

b) The future is also used to express probability in sentences like:

quanti anni avrà? – non so, ne avrà una trentina
how old do you think he/she is? – I don't know, maybe thirty

che ore saranno?
what time could it be?

guadagnerà al massimo come te
he/she can't possibly earn more than you

dove mai sarà Gabriella?
where on earth can Gabriella be?

8 Future perfect

a) This compound tense is used to describe what someone will have done or will have been doing in the future or to describe something that will have happened in the future:

allora avrò sicuramente finito
I will definitely have finished by then

quando lo avrai visto, cambierai idee
when you see it, you will change your mind

b) The future perfect can also express probability in sentences like:

è partito subito: avrà avuto fretta
he left straight away: he must have been in a hurry

non è ancora arrivata: che cosa le sarà successo?
she hasn't arrived yet: what can have happened to her?

9 Present perfect and past perfect progressive

a) The present must be used instead of the perfect to describe actions which started in the past and have continued until the present:

abita qui da tre anni
he/she's been living here for three years

lo aspetta da stamattina
he/she's been waiting for him since this morning

Note that the preposition da (since) is used where the English uses 'for'. The sentence ha abitato qui per tre anni is also possible, but it means 'he lived here for three years' (and now he lives somewhere else).

b) The imperfect must be used instead of the pluperfect to describe an action which had started in the past and was still going on at a given time:

quando ti incontrai, studiavi l'italiano da due mesi
when I met you, you had been studying Italian for two months

aspettava da tre ore quando siamo arrivati
he/she had been waiting for three hours when we arrived

The preposition da (since) is used where the English uses 'for'. A sentence like aveva studiato l'italiano per due mesi is also possible, but it would mean 'he had studied Italian for two months' (but was no longer studying it).

 G THE SUBJUNCTIVE

The subjunctive in Italian has four tenses: present, imperfect, perfect and pluperfect. *For the formation of these tenses see p 114, 115 and pp 119-20.*

penso che Mario studi molto
I think Mario studies hard *(present)*

penso che abbia studiato molto
I think he studied hard *(perfect)*

pensavo che studiasse molto
I thought he studied hard
    (imperfect)

pensavo che avesse studiato molto
I thought he had studied hard
    (pluperfect)

In Italian, unlike English, the subjunctive is used extensively. It is used in both main and subordinate clauses. In subordinate clauses a choice between the subjunctive and the indicative is often possible. When a formal register is sought, the subjunctive is always to be preferred whereas the indicative may be found in colloquial and regional varieties of Italian. It should also be remembered that the indicative expresses a greater degree of certainty than the subjunctive.

In many of the following examples the use of the indicative would also be possible, but often with a difference in implication. For example:

era il solo cavallo che poteva vincere *(indicative)*
it was the only horse that could win *(a fact given the circumstances)*

era il solo cavallo che potesse vincere *(subjunctive)*
it was the only horse that could win *(in my opinion)*

Sometimes, however, there is little difference between the use of the indicative and the subjunctive, the latter simply expressing a higher level of formality:

temo che farà freddo domani
temo che faccia freddo domani
I'm afraid it will be cold tomorrow

1 Use of the subjunctive in main clauses

The subjunctive is used in main clauses to express a wish or a doubt:

siate felici!
may you be happy!

che abbia mangiato troppo?
I wonder if I have eaten too much

It is also used to form the polite form (for lei/loro) of the imperative:

vada piano
go slowly

It is also used in exclamations and concessive expressions:

sapessi che divertimento!
if you knew what fun it is/was!

sia ricco o no
be he rich or not

2 Use of the subjunctive in subordinate clauses

The subjunctive can be used after the following:

a) Verbs of emotion:

essere contento/scontento che	to be pleased/displeased that
essere felice/infelice che	to be happy/unhappy that
aver paura che	to be afraid that
rammaricarsi che	to regret that
rincrescere che	to regret that
essere sorpreso/stupito che	to be surprised that
stupirsi che	to be surprised that
essere spiacente che	to be sorry that
temere che	to fear that

erano contenti che nevicasse
they were pleased that it snowed

avevano paura che fosse troppo tardi
they were worried that it was too late

b) Verbs of wishing, willing, allowing and preventing:

augurarsi che	to wish (that)
impedire che	to prevent
lasciare che	to let
permettere che	to allow
preferire che	to prefer
sperare che	to hope
volere che	to want

spero che tu abbia un po' di fortuna
I hope that you will be lucky

si auguravano che l'aereo partisse presto
they wished that the plane would leave soon

Note that in English such verbs are often used in the following types of construction: verb of willing + object + infinitive, eg *I'd like you to listen*; this type of construction is impossible in Italian, where a subjunctive clause has to be used:

lasciò che finissero di parlare
he/she allowed them to finish talking

vorrebbe che tu lo andassi a trovare più spesso
he/she would like you to go and visit him more often

c) Impersonal constructions (expressing necessity, possibility, doubt, denial, preference):

basta che	it is enough (that)
è bene/male che	it is a good/bad thing that
bisogna che	it is necessary (that), ... must
conviene che	one had better
è facile/difficile che	it is likely/unlikely that
è meglio/peggio che	it is better/worse that
è naturale che	it is natural that
è un peccato che	it is a pity (that)
è possibile/impossibile che	it is possible/impossible that
è preferibile che	it is preferable (that)
è probabile/improbabile che	it is likely/unlikely that
sembra che	it seems (that)
è strano che	it is odd that
è utile/inutile che	it is useful/useless that
vale la pena che	it is worth

è inutile che tu ti preoccupi per quell'esame
it is pointless for you to worry about the exam

converrà che usciamo presto per trovare un posteggio
we had better leave early to find a parking space

Note that in English, such expressions are also used in the following type of construction: impersonal expression + (for) + object + infinitive. A subjunctive clause must be used in Italian to convey the same meaning:

è importante che tu abbia successo
it's important for you to succeed

vale la pena che stiri i tuoi calzoni?
is it worth my ironing your trousers?

d) Some verbs of knowledge, perception and affirmation, in particular in the negative and interrogative:

(non) sapere se	(not) to know whether
(non) credere che	(not) to believe, think that
(non) vedere come	(not) to see how
(non) affermare che	(not) to assert that
(non) dire che	(not) to say that

non so se sia già ora di cena
I don't know whether it's dinner time yet

non vedo come possa trovarlo attraente
I don't see how she can find him attractive

credi che l'autobus sia già passato?
do you think the bus has already gone?

e) Verbs of thought, doubt and denial:

pensare che	to think that
parere/sembrare che	to seem that
dubitare che	to doubt that
negare che	to deny that

dubito che si ricordi di passare in tintoria
I don't think he'll remember to go to the dry cleaner's

pensavo che fossero partiti per le vacanze
I thought they had left for their holidays

f) Verbs of asking followed by indirect questions:

chiedere se   to ask whether
domandare se   to ask whether
domandò se lì facesse freddo
he/she asked if it was cold there

mi chiedo se siano soldi ben spesi
I ask myself whether it is worth the money

g) **attendere che/aspettare che** (to wait until, to wait for (someone to do something)):

aspettiamo che sia di buon umore
let's wait until he/she is in a good mood

h) Some subordinating conjunctions and subordinating expressions (note that the following are ALWAYS followed by the subjunctive):

affinché/perché	so that
benché/sebbene/quantunque	(al)though
nonostante che	in spite of
purché/a patto che/a condizione che	provided that
nel caso che/qualora/caso mai	in case
come se	as if
senza che	without
di modo che/in maniera che	so that
a meno che (non)* ...	unless
prima che (non)* ...	before
per paura che (non)* ...	for fear that

*Note that in these three expressions, **non** does not have a negative meaning and is not translated in English

telefono perché tu sappia che l'aereo è in ritardo
I'm calling to let you know that the plane is late

sebbene sia passato un anno ne parla sempre
although a year has gone by he/she still talks about it all the time

ecco il mio numero, qualora le servisse
here's my number in case you need it

la salutò come se la conoscesse
he/she greeted her as if he/she knew her

laverò le lenzuola domani, a meno che non cambi il tempo
I'll wash the sheets tomorrow unless the weather changes

voglio vedere dei miglioramenti prima che finisca il trimestre
I want to see some improvements before the term is over

camminiamo in punta dei piedi in modo che non ci sentano
let's go on tiptoe so that they don't hear us

Note that di modo che/in maniera che (so that) take the indicative and not the subjunctive when used to express a result as opposed to a purpose:

fece rumore, di modo che lo sentirono
he made a noise, so that they heard him

Note too that perché takes the indicative when it means 'because'.

i) Indefinite adjectives and pronouns introducing clauses:

chiunque	**qualunque**
whoever	whichever
qualsiasi	**qualunque cosa**
whichever	whatever
chiunque lo pensi sbaglia	
whoever thinks that is wrong	
qualsiasi cosa tu dica avrà gran peso	
whatever you say will carry great weight	

j) The second term of comparison in comparative clauses:

è meno serena di quanto sperassi
she is less calm than I had hoped

k) A superlative of an adjective or the words primo (first), ultimo (last), solo/unico (only) followed by a relative clause:

è il ragazzo più testardo che conosca
he is the most stubborn boy I know

l) Negative or indefinite pronouns or adjectives like nessuno (no one, no), niente/nulla (nothing), qualcuno (somebody) in dependent relative clauses:

non c'è niente che mi commuova tanto
there is nothing that moves me so much

non c'è nessuna probabilità che siano liberati
there is no chance that they will be freed

cercano qualcuno che faccia da interprete
they are looking for somebody to act as interpreter

m) che when it introduces subordinate clauses which precede the main clause:

che sia brava lo so già
that she is capable I already know

n) *For the use of the subjunctive in if-clauses see* p 158.

3 Restrictions on the use of the subjunctive

If the subject of the main clause and that of the subordinate clause are the same, then the subjunctive is replaced by a construction with the infinitive. The infinitive can be introduced by di, by no preposition at all or by a:

a) di + infinitive replaces the subjunctive after:

    i) verbs of emotion:

        furono contenti di partire   **sei felice di rivederla?**
        they were happy to leave   are you happy to see her again?

        avevo paura di essere in ritardo
        I was worried that I was late/about being late

    ii) some verbs of wishing, willing, allowing:

        spero di finire presto questo lavoro
        I hope to finish this job soon

        si augurarono di non rivederlo più
        they wished never to see him again

iii) verbs of knowledge, perception and affirmation:

non credo di pretendere troppo
I don't think that I'm expecting too much

non pensavo di essere l'unico
I didn't think I was the only one

iv) verbs of thought, doubt and denial:

pensate di passare inosservati?
do you think you can go unnoticed?

negavano di essere terroristi
they denied that they were terrorists

v) attendere, aspettare:

attendevano di passare la dogana
they were waiting to go through Customs

vi) some conjunctions and subordinating expressions:

si pettinò prima di uscire
he/she combed his/her hair before going out

spensero la luce per paura di esser visti
they turned the light off for fear of being seen

voleva dimagrire per mettersi il due pezzi
she wanted to lose weight to be able to wear a bikini

parlò senza balbettare
he/she spoke without stuttering

b) The infinitive without any linking preposition replaces the subjunctive after:

i) **bisogna, basta** and most impersonal verbs and expressions:

è inutile lamentarsi adesso
it is no use complaining now

ii) some verbs of wishing, willing, allowing:

preferisco nuotare all'alba
I prefer to swim at dawn

volevano concludere l'affare
they wanted to clinch the deal

iii) **se** introducing indirect questions:

   non sapevo se ridere o piangere
   I didn't know whether to laugh or cry

c) The infinitive is preceded by the preposition **a** after **primo** (first), **ultimo** (last), **solo/unico** (only):

   è stata la prima ad andarsene
   she was the first to leave

4 Sequence of tenses with the subjunctive

Two considerations determine which tense of the subjunctive is used in subordinate clauses. These are:

❏ the tense used in the main clause
❏ the time relationship between the main clause and the subordinate clause, that is whether the subordinate clause describes an action which is contemporary with the action in the main clause, which follows the action in the main clause or which is previous to the action in the main clause.

a) When the verb in the main clause is in the present or future indicative, the tense in the subordinate clause will be:

   i) the present subjunctive to describe a contemporary or a following action:

   penso che oggi studino in biblioteca
   I think they are studying in the library today

   spero che la prossima settimana tu stia meglio
   I hope that you feel better next week

   farò finta che tu non sia qui
   I'll pretend you're not here

   ii) the perfect subjunctive to describe a previous action:

   la polizia cerca testimoni che abbiano notato la macchina
   the police are looking for witnesses who noticed the car

   chiederà come siano riusciti a spendere tanto
   he/she will ask how they managed to spend so much

b) When the verb of the main clause is in the imperfect indicative, past historic, perfect or pluperfect, the tense used in the subordinate clause will be:

i) the imperfect subjunctive to describe a contemporary action:

pensavo che fossero stanchi per il viaggio
I thought that they were tired because of the journey

gli sembrò che il clima fosse ideale
he thought that the climate was ideal

hanno creduto che venisse da lontano
they thought that he/she came from far away

avevano cercato una casa che avesse un bel giardino
they had looked for a house that had a nice garden

ii) the pluperfect subjunctive to describe a previous action:

cercavano qualcuno che avesse lavorato in quella fabbrica
they were looking for someone who had worked in that factory

chiese se le avessero già spedito il pacco
she asked whether they had already sent the parcel to her

**hanno sbagliato strada nonostante avessero ricevuto istruzioni
   dettagliate**
they took the wrong road in spite of having received detailed
   instructions

non era riuscito a scoprire se avessero telefonato o no
he couldn't ascertain whether they had phoned or not

iii) the past conditional to describe a following action (*see* pp 156-8):

speravo che avebbero trovato un lavoro
I hoped that they would find a job

 H THE CONDITIONAL

The conditional describes an action that could happen (or might have happened) under certain conditions. It has two tenses: present and past. *For the forms of the conditional see* p 113.

1 Use of the present conditional

a) To describe an action that could take place in the present or the future:

oggi risolverei quel problema in modo diverso
today I would solve the problem in a different way

b) To express a wish or desire:

vorrei un caffè
I would like a coffee

potrei cucinare la torta domani?
could I bake the cake tomorrow?

c) To express a doubt concerning a present or future action:

che cosa dovrei fare?
what should I do?

d) To express an action, situation or occurrence which would be possible on certain conditions:

se avessi tempo, andrei volentieri al cinema
if I had the time, I would really like to go to the cinema

e) To express a certainty:

non farei mai una cosa simile!
I would never do such a thing!

f) To express discreetly a personal opinion:

penso che sarebbe una buona idea
I think it would be a good idea

g) With reported speech:

dice che accetterebbe la vostra proposta
he/she says he/she would accept your proposal

h) To express the possibility that something is happening in the present:

secondo questo articolo gli ostaggi sarebbero a Beirut
according to this article the hostages are in Beirut

2 Use of the past conditional

a) To describe an action that might have taken place in the past:

avrei potuto cucinare la torta ieri sera
I could have baked the cake yesterday evening

b) To express an unfulfilled wish or desire in the past:

avrei voluto un caffè
I would have liked a coffee

c) To express doubt concerning a past action:

che cosa avrei dovuto fare?
what should I have done?

d) To express a past action, situation or occurrence which would have been possible on certain conditions:

avrebbe accettato la proposta se avessero cancellato il paragrafo 3
he/she would have accepted the proposal if clause 3 had been dropped

e) To express a sense of surprise or disbelief about a past action:

non avrei mai fatto una cosa simile!
I would never have done such a thing!

f) To express discreetly a personal opinon about a past action:

penso che sarebbe stata una buona idea
I think it would have been a good idea

g) With reported speech:

disse che avrei accettato la tua proposta
he/she said he/she would accept your proposal

Note that in this case Italian, unlike English, must use the past conditional.

h) To express the possibility that something was happening in the past:

secondo quell'articolo gli ostaggi sarebbero stati a Beirut
according to that article the hostages were in Beirut

Note

- When 'would' suggests resolve, it is expressed by volere:

  non mi volle ascoltare
  he/she would not listen to me

- When 'would' suggests repeated action, it is conveyed by the imperfect indicative:

  d'estate innaffiava il giardino ogni sera
  in summer he/she would water the garden every evening

- When 'should' means 'ought to', it is expressed by dovere:

  dovresti fare più sport
  you should do more sport

3 Sequence of tenses with the conditional

a) When the verb in the main clause is in the present (or future) indicative, the tense used in the subordinate clause will be:

   i) the present conditional to describe a contemporary or a subsequent action:

   penso che adesso verrebbero volentieri
   I think that they would be pleased to come now

   credo che Carlo ci potrebbe andare domani
   I think Carlo could go there tomorrow

   ii) the past conditional to describe a previous action:

   penso che avrebbe dovuto farlo
   I think he/she should have done it

b) When the verb in the main clause is in the imperfect indicative, past historic, perfect or pluperfect, the tense used in the subordinate clause will be:

   i) the imperfect subjunctive to describe a contemporary action (*see* p 154)

ii) the pluperfect subjunctive to describe a previous action (*see* p 154)

iii) the past conditional to describe a subsequent action:

pensavo che lo avresti finito in tempo
I thought you would finish it in time

4 Use of tenses in if-clauses

a) If the main clause refers to the present or to the future, the verb in the main clause uses the present conditional and the verb in the conditional clause (if-clause) uses:

i) the imperfect subjunctive, if the action it expresses is contemporary with the action in the main clause:

se lo sapessi te lo direi
I would tell you if I knew

se non guardassi la TV avresti tempo per leggere
if you didn't watch TV you would have time to read

ii) the pluperfect subjunctive, if the action it expresses is previous to the action in the main clause:

se avessi studiato di più, ora passeresti l'esame
if you had studied more, you would pass the exam

se ieri non avessi guardato la TV, ora non saprei tutto sull'argomento
if I hadn't watched TV yesterday, I wouldn't now know all there is to know on this subject

b) If the main clause refers to the past, the verb in the main clause is in the past conditional and the verb in the 'if' clause uses the pluperfect subjunctive:

se lo avessi saputo te lo avrei detto
I would have told you if I had known

se fosse stato più giovane avrebbe dormito in tenda
if he had been younger he would have slept in the tent

Note that Italian never uses the conditional in a clause with **se** meaning 'if'.

I THE IMPERATIVE

1 Definition

The imperative is used to give commands, or polite instructions,
or to make requests or suggestions. These can be positive ('do!') or
negative ('don't!') and they can refer to the present or to the future:

vieni subito qua! come here straight away!	**non aver paura!** don't be afraid!
chiedete scusa! apologize!	**andiamo!** let's go!
non continuate! don't go on!	**non esca!** don't go out!
camminate sul marciapiede walk on the pavement	**all'incrocio girate a destra** turn right at the crossroads

2 Forms

a) The forms of the imperative for the tu and voi forms are identical
to those of the present indicative with the exception of the tu
form of first conjugation (-are) verbs:

	-ARE VERBS	-ERE VERBS	-IRE VERBS
singular			
tu	parla	credi	dormi
plural			
voi	parlate	credete	dormite

VERBS

b) To express an imperative in the first person plural (noi) and in the polite form (lei, loro) the corresponding forms of the present subjunctive are used:

corriamo! *(noi)*
let's run!

continui sempre dritto! *(lei)*
carry straight on!

vada pure *(lei)*
by all means go

si accomodino, prego *(loro)*
please be seated

abbiano pazienza *(loro)*
be patient

3 Irregular imperatives

The two auxiliary verbs (essere and avere) use the following forms:

	singular	*plural*	
ESSERE	sii	siate	be
AVERE	abbi	abbiate	have

The following common verbs have some irregular forms which are different from the present indicative:

	singular	*plural*	
ANDARE	va'	andate	go
DARE	da'	date	give
DIRE	di'	dite	say
FARE	fa'	fate	do, make
SAPERE	sappi	sappiate	you must know
STARE	sta'	state	be

4 Negative commands

In negative commands non precedes the affirmative forms of the verb. In the tu form, however, non is followed by the infinitive.

2ND PERSON SING	2ND PERSON PLURAL	
non mangiare	non mangiate	do not eat
non prendere	non prendete	do not take
non finire	non finite	do not finish

2ND PERSON SING POLITE	2ND PERSON PLURAL POLITE	
non mangi *(lei)*	non mangiate *(voi)*	do not eat
	non mangino *(loro)*	

For the use of voi *as the plural polite form see* **p 76.**

1ST PERSON PLURAL	
non mangiamo	let's not eat

5 The imperative with object pronouns (excluding the polite form)

In positive commands, object pronouns and ci (vi) and ne (*see* p 82) come after the verb and are attached to it.

credimi!
believe me
(singular 'you' form)

mandatele un assegno
send her a cheque
(plural 'you' form)

spiegale di che si tratta
explain to her what it is about
(singular 'you' form)

andateci voi!
you go there!
(plural 'you' form)

scriviamogli subito
let's write to him straight away

Note the following points:

i) loro comes after the verb but is written separately:

prendi loro un gelato
get them an ice cream

ii) after the five imperatives va', da', di', fa', sta', pronouns, with the exception of gli, double their initial consonant:

dimmi la verità	**stalle vicino**
tell me the truth	stay close to her

But: **fagli compagnia**
keep him company

iii) with a negative command the object pronouns can either follow the verb or be placed between non and the verb:

non raccontarmi storie	**non pensateci più**
non mi raccontare storie	**non ci pensate più**
don't tell me stories	don't think about it any more

6 Polite form – commands with object pronouns

Object pronouns and ci (vi) and ne always precede polite form commands:

gli offra un caffè	**mi faccia il piacere!**
offer him/them a cup of coffee	do me a favour!

non mi faccia aspettare
don't keep me waiting

Note, however, that loro follows the verb:

dica loro di prenotare un tavolo
tell them to book a table

7 Imperative of reflexive verbs

The position of the reflexive pronouns of reflexive verbs is the same as that of object pronouns:

alzati *(tu)*	**si alzi** *(lei)*
get up	get up
non fidatevi di lui *(voi)*	**pettinatevi** *(voi)*
don't trust him	comb your hair
fermiamoci qua *(noi)*	
let's stop here	

8 Alternatives to the imperative

The infinitive is often used instead of the imperative in written instructions, such as signposts and recipes:

non fumare
no smoking

non sostare
no stopping

lasciare libero il passo
keep clear

 THE INFINITIVE

1 Definition and forms

The infinitive is the basic form of the verb. It is recognized by its ending, which is found in three forms: **-are** for the first conjugation, **-ere** for the second and **-ire** for the third:

parlare	**credere**	**sentire**
to speak	to believe	to hear/to feel

Note the following points:

i) The endings **-are**, **-ere**, **-ire** give the verb the meaning 'to ...'. The Italian infinitive will, however, often be translated by a verb form ending in '-ing' (see below).

ii) A few common verbs have irregular infinitives, among them:

tradurre	**produrre**	**condurre**	**porre**
to translate	to produce	to lead	to put
imporre	**proporre**	**comporre**	
to impose	to propose	to compose	

2 Tenses

The infinitive has two tenses: the present infinitive and the past infinitive. The past infinitive is formed by adding the past participle of the verb to the infinitive of the appropriate auxiliary (*see* pp 118-26):

PRESENT		PAST	
amare	to love	aver(e) amato	to have loved
arrivare	to arrive	esser(e) arrivato	to have arrived
alzarsi	to get up	essersi alzato	to have got up

Note that the final -e of avere and essere can be omitted.

3 Uses of the infinitive

a) *After a preposition*

The infinitive can be used after some prepositions (prima di, dopo, senza, al fine di, invece di, tra, con, per *etc*):

prima di protestare
before complaining

dopo aver mangiato
after eating

invece di affrettarsi
instead of hurrying

senza pettinarsi
without combing one's hair

per sentirsi bene
in order to feel well

Note that dopo is always followed by the past infinitive.

b) *After a verb*

There are three main constructions when a verb is followed by an infinitive (*for lists of the main verbs in each category see pp 206-16*):

i) verbs followed by the infinitive with no linking preposition:

Many of these verbs belong to the following groups:

❏ modal verbs:

dovere	must, to have to
potere	can, to be able to
volere	will, to want to
vuoi fare una doccia?	**devo lavare i piatti**
do you want to have a shower?	I have to do the dishes

❏ verbs of seeing, hearing:

vedere	to see
guardare	to watch
sentire	to hear
ascoltare	to listen to

di domenica ascoltavo le campane suonare
on Sundays I listened to the bells ringing

mi hai guardata ballare?
did you watch me dance?

❏ most impersonal verbs:

bisogna pagare   **occorre pensarci sopra**
you have to pay   it's necessary to think it over

conviene accettare quell'offerta
it's better to accept that offer

❏ impersonal expressions with essere:

è sempre piacevole parlare   è difficile trovarlo a casa
  con te   it's difficult to find him at home
it's always pleasant to talk
  to you

❏ verbs of liking and disliking:

amare	to love, to be fond of
adorare	to adore, to love
detestare	to hate
piacere	to like
preferire	to prefer

amo ascoltare musica classica   preferiscono viaggiare di notte
I like listening to classical music   they prefer travelling by night

ii) verbs with the linking preposition a:

Many of these verbs belong to the following groups:

❏ verbs of motion:

andare	to go
venire	to come
entrare	to go/come in
uscire	to go/come out
salire	to go/come up
scendere	to go/come down

salga a vedere come sta   **vieni a vedere**
go up and see how he/she is   come and see

va' a comprare il giornale
go and buy a newspaper

Note that in English these verbs may be linked by 'and' to the verb that follows; 'and' is not expressed in Italian.

❏ verbs of beginning, continuing, preparing:

cominciare	to begin
iniziare	to begin
continuare	to continue
prepararsi	to get ready

all'alba gli uccelli cominciarono a cantare
at dawn the birds began to sing

si preparavano a suonare
they were getting ready to play

❏ verbs of teaching and learning:

apprendere	to learn
imparare	to learn
insegnare	to teach

imparò a cavalcare in poche lezioni
he/she learned to ride in a few lessons

ci insegnò a parlare italiano
he/she taught us to speak Italian

❏ verbs of compulsion:

furono costretti a consegnare il denaro
they were forced to hand over the money

❏ the expressions **far bene, far male** *etc*:

hai fatto bene a vendere la casa
you were right to sell your house

❏ **essere** followed by a numeral or by **solo, ultimo**:

furono i primi a scusarsi
they were the first to apologize

sei il solo a non sentire la sveglia
you are the only one who can't hear the alarm clock

iii) verbs with the linking preposition **di**:
These include the majority of Italian verbs. Many belong to the following groups:

❏ verbs of hope, belief, knowledge:

credo di sbagliare   **sapeva di essere in ritardo**
I believe I am wrong   he/she knew he/she was late

speravano di tornare in Inghilterra
they hoped to go back to England

❏ verbs of commanding:

ordinarono di cessare il fuoco
they ordered a ceasefire

❏ verbs of saying, asking:

chiesero di essere svegliati alle sei
they asked to be woken up at six

❏ verbs of doubt, uncertainty:

dubito di avere abbastanza tempo
I doubt I'll have enough time

❏ verbs of surprise, fear, emotion:

si stupì di vedere un cervo vicino alla strada
he/she was surprised to see a deer by the roadside

❏ verbs of trying:

cerca di non macchiare la tovaglia
try not to stain the tablecloth

ci sforzeremo di finire questo lavoro in tempo
we'll try to finish this job on time

Note that the verbs **astenersi** (to abstain from) and **contenersi** (to refrain from) are followed by the linking preposition **da**:

durante il giorno si astengono dal mangiare e dal bere
they abstain from eating and drinking during the day

c) *After an adjective*

There are three main constructions when an adjective is followed by an infinitive:

i) some common adjectives with the linking preposition **a**:

abituato	used
adatto	suitable
autorizzato	authorized, licensed
contrario	against, opposed
deciso	determined
disposto	willing
inutile	useless
lento	slow
pronto	ready
utile	useful

sono pronta a partire   **è deciso a vincere l'incontro**
I'm ready to leave   he's determined to win the match

quel negozio è autorizzato a vendere vini e liquori
that shop is licensed to sell wines and spirits

ii) some common adjectives with the linking preposition di:

ansioso	anxious
bramoso	eager
certo	certain
contento	happy
curioso	curious
degno	worthy
desideroso	keen
felice	happy, glad
impaziente	impatient
indegno	unworthy
infelice	unhappy
lieto	happy
scontento	dissatisfied
sicuro	certain
stanco	tired

felice di conoscerla!
pleased to meet you!

erano impazienti di chiarire l'equivoco
they were anxious to clear up the misunderstanding

siamo desiderosi di ricevere vostre notizie
we are keen to hear your news

iii) some common adjectives with the linking preposition da:

bello	beautiful
buffo	funny
differente	different
difficile	difficult
divertente	amusing
facile	easy
gradevole	pleasant
sgradevole	unpleasant

è facile da usare　　　　　　**Pietro è difficile da capire**
it's easy to use　　　　　　　　Pietro is difficult to understand

Note that in constructions with **essere**, adjectives can also be followed by **da** + infinitive to convey the idea of 'to a very high degree':

è simpatico da morire
he's really really nice

d) *After a noun*

There are three possible constructions when a noun is followed by an infinitive:

i) **da** is used in the majority of cases and conveys the idea of something to be done:

hanno una casa da vendere
they have a house for sale

ci ha mostrato la strada da seguire
he/she showed us the road to take

ci sono solo tre libri da leggere per questo corso
there are only three books to read for this course

ii) **di** is used to define something more closely:

non è il momento di disturbarlo
now is not the time to disturb him

avevano piacere di trovarsi ogni tanto
they were happy to meet from time to time

iii) **per** is used to express an aim or a purpose:

i soldi per andare all'estero
the money to go abroad

Gabriele sta risparmiando per comprarsi il motorino
Gabriele's saving up to buy a moped

e) **fare + infinitive**

fare is followed by an infinitive without any linking preposition to express the idea of 'making someone do something' or 'having something done':

fa' pulire quel tappeto	**farò prenotare una cuccetta**
have that carpet cleaned	I'll book a sleeper

mi ha fatto aspettare per delle ore!
he/she kept me waiting for hours!

Note that when both verbs (fare and the following infinitive) have an object in English, the object of fare becomes indirect in Italian:

fecero cambiare le lenzuola alla cameriera
they got the chambermaid to change the sheets

f) **stare per + infinitive**

This construction expresses 'to be about to', 'to be on the point of':

stavo per uscire quando si è messo a piovere
I was about to go out when it started to rain

stanno per trasmettere la partita
they are about to broadcast the match

K PARTICIPLES

1 The present participle

a) *Formation*

The present participle is formed by adding the endings -ante (1st conjugation) or -ente (2nd and 3rd conjugations) to the stem of the verb. The plural is formed by replacing -e with -i:

parlante/i	**credente**/i	**udente**/i
speaking	believing	hearing

b) *Use as a verb*

The present participle is used less frequently in Italian than in English. English present participles are often conveyed by the gerund (*see* p 176) or by the infinitive (*see* p 163). The following present participles are commonly used with a verbal function:

attestante	testifying	indicante	indicating
concernente	concerning	manifestante	revealing
contenente	containing	proveniente	deriving
eccedente	exceeding	rappresentante	representing
formante	forming		

un camion proveniente da Trieste
a lorry coming from Trieste

un certificato attestante la sua frequenza alle lezioni
a certificate testifying his/her class attendance

due valigie contenenti i loro regali di nozze
two suitcases containing their wedding presents

Note that manifestante and rappresentante are mainly used as nouns:

il manifestante
the demonstrator

il rappresentante esclusivo
the sole agent

The present participle must be used with caution. When in doubt it is better to use a relative clause:

un uccello che canta
a bird singing

c) *Use as an adjective or as a noun*

Present participles are most frequently used as adjectives:

frustrante	*(adjective)*	frustrating
crescente	*(adjective)*	growing

Note that the formation of a few participles is irregular:

nutriente	*(adjective)*	nourishing
ubbidiente	*(adjective)*	obedient
seguente	*(adjective)*	following

Some present participles can be both a noun and an adjective:

| **corrente** | *(noun)* | stream | *(adjective)* | running |
| **docente** | *(noun)* | teacher | *(adjective)* | teaching |

Note that some present participles originate from verbs which are no longer used in contemporary Italian:

| **mittente** | *(noun)* | sender |
| **abbiente** | *(adjective)* | well-off |

2 The past participle

a) *Formation*

The past participle is formed by adding the endings below to the stem of the verb. The feminine and plural endings of the past participle are the same as adjective endings:

1st conjugation	-ato/a/i/e
2nd conjugation	-uto/a/i/e
3rd conjugation	-ito/a/i/e
mangiato/a/i/e	venduto/a/i/e partito/a/i/e

Note that the formation of a large number of past participles is irregular and these must be learned individually.

b) *Use*

The past participle is used in compound tenses and in the passive:

Mario ha scritto una poesia
Mario wrote a poem

quell'edificio è stato costruito in tre mesi
that building was built in three months

3 Agreement of the past participle

a) When the auxiliary is **essere**, the past participle agrees with the subject:

Cesare è tornato in Italia   **Simona è partita per Napoli**
Cesare went back to Italy   Simona has left for Naples

i regali sono stati divisi equamente
the presents were divided equally

dove sono andate quelle studentesse?
where have those students gone?

b) When the auxiliary is **avere** and the direct object is not expressed, the past participle does not agree with the subject:

Donatella ha insegnato qui per due anni
Donatella has taught here for two years

c) When the auxiliary is **avere** and the direct object is expressed *after* the participle, no agreement takes place:

Michela ha comprato tre libri
Michela bought three books

d) When the auxiliary is **avere** and the direct object is expressed *before* the participle, agreement is optional (but the second form is much more common):

i libri che Nadia ha comprati
i libri che Nadia ha comprato
the books Nadia bought

e) When the auxiliary is **avere**, and the direct object is one of the personal pronouns **lo, la, li, le** and precedes the verb, the past participle agrees with the direct object:

lo ha comprato ieri *(il libro)*
he/she bought it yesterday *(the book)*

le ha comprate oggi *(le banane)*
he/she bought them today *(the bananas)*

f) When the auxiliary is avere, and the direct object is one of the pronouns mi, ti, ci, vi and ne (partitive) and precedes the verb, agreement with the direct object is optional:

mi dispiace, Silvia, se ti ho disturbata
mi dispiace, Silvia, se ti ho disturbato
I'm sorry if I bothered you, Silvia

ha mangiato della pasta   **ne ha mangiata/mangiata**
he/she ate some pasta   he/she ate some of it

Note, however, that if there is another qualifying word in the same sentence which shows agreement then the past participle *must* also agree:

ne ha mangiata troppa
he/she ate too much (of it)

g) With reflexive verbs the past participle can agree with either the subject or the object:

Lucia si è lavata le mani
Lucia si è lavate le mani
Lucia washed her hands

h) When used as an adjective, the past participle always agrees:

una camicia stirata   **un animale ammalato**
an ironed shirt   a sick animal

delle stampe colorate   **tre piatti rotti**
some coloured prints   three broken plates

L THE GERUND

1 The present gerund

a) *Forms*

The present gerund is formed by adding to the stem of each conjugation the endings -ando (-are verbs) or -endo (-ere and -ire verbs):

parlando	credendo	aprendo
speaking	believing	opening

The present gerund is invariable and there are no irregular forms.

b) *Use*

The present gerund is used to express the mode of an action (ie it has an adverbial function). It refers to the same time as the main clause and usually to the same subject:

passeggiando per il parco ho incontrato Marina
I met Marina when I was walking in the park

arriverà lì prima prendendo la circonvallazione
you will get there more quickly by taking the ring road

si fece male cadendo **sbagliando si impara** *(proverb)*
he hurt himself falling   one learns by making mistakes

Note that the gerund is never preceded by a preposition.

c) *Special constructions with the present gerund*

i) stare + gerund:

This construction suggests a continuous action:

sto cucinando
I'm cooking

stava facendo la doccia quando suonò il telefono
he/she was having a shower when the phone rang

Note that the imperfect is the only past tense with which this construction can be used.

ii) andare + gerund:

This suggests repeated, methodical action:

andava raccontando storie incredibili
he/she went around telling incredible tales

2 The perfect gerund

a) *Forms*

The perfect gerund is formed with the gerund of the auxiliary **essere** or **avere** as appropriate (*see* pp 118-26) followed by the past participle of the verb:

essendo stato	**avendo avuto**	**avendo amato**
having been	having had	having loved

essendosi alzato	**essendo arrivato**
having got up	having arrived

When the perfect gerund is conjugated with **essere** the past participle, but not the gerund, agrees with the subject.

b) *Use*

The perfect gerund refers to a time which precedes that of the main clause, but its use is not very common. It usually refers to the same subject:

Gianni scappò, avendo sentito la sirena
Gianni ran away, having heard the siren

THE PASSIVE

1 Formation

The passive is used with transitive verbs when the subject does not perform the action but is subjected to it, eg:

active: the mayor opened the exhibition
passive: the exhibition was opened by the mayor

Passive tenses are formed with the corresponding tense of the verb **essere** ('to be', as in English) followed by the past participle of the verb:

sono stato invitato
I was invited

a) The past participle must agree with the subject:

quella ragazza è stata licenziata
that girl was dismissed

gli inquilini sono stati sfrattati
the tenants have been evicted

le attrici sono state intervistate
the actresses have been interviewed

b) Prepositions with passive verbs:

When the agent or the doer of the action is mentioned, it is preceded by **da** (by):

active: **Montale ha scritto questa poesia**
Montale wrote this poem

passive: **questa poesia è stata scritta da Montale**
this poem was written *by* Montale

2 Alternative forms

a) In non-compound tenses the verb **venire** can replace **essere**:

oggi la cataratta viene operata col laser
nowadays cataracts are operated on with a laser

il digestivo viene generalmente servito dopo cena
a liqueur is usually served after dinner

b) The verb andare can also be used instead of dover essere, meaning 'must be':

le promesse vanno mantenute
promises must be kept

il presidente va servito per primo
the president must be served first

c) The si passivante

The passive can also be formed in Italian by placing the pronoun si before the third person singular or plural of verbs in the active form:

in quella libreria i libri si vendevano (= erano venduti) a metà prezzo
in that bookshop books used to be sold at half-price

in Italia si vendono (= sono vendute) ancora molte pellicce
in Italy many fur coats are still sold

col pesce si serve (= è servito) di solito il vino bianco
white wine is usually served with fish

Note

Try not to confuse the si passivante with the impersonal si, which is only used in the third person singular (*see* p 135). In the following examples to use the singular si vede instead of the plural would be wrong:

oggi si vedono più programmi televisivi che nel passato
nowadays people watch more TV than in the past

da questa finestra si vedono le colline
from this window you can see the hills

For the other uses of si, *see* p 91.

---

3 Verbs with indirect objects

English passive sentences like 'I was taught Italian' cannot be translated literally into Italian, since the Italian verb 'to teach' takes an indirect object. Italian can translate an English passive sentence literally only if the direct object of an active sentence can become the subject of a passive sentence (eg 'I saw *him*' = 'he was seen by me'). One possible translation of 'I was taught Italian' would therefore be **mi è stato insegnato l'italiano**. The subject pronoun has become an indirect object. In reality, however, Italian is much more likely to express this idea without using a passive at all:

mi hanno insegnato l'italiano
they taught me Italian/I was taught Italian

 N MODAL AUXILIARY VERBS

The three modal auxiliary verbs (expressing obligation, probability, ability, wish) are **DOVERE**, **POTERE** and **VOLERE**. They are always followed by an infinitive.

1 DOVERE (*conjugation* p 192)

expresses:

❏ obligation, necessity
❏ probability
❏ intention, expectation

a) *Obligation, necessity*

dovete essere in ufficio per le otto
you must be in the office by eight o'clock

ho dovuto rispondere subito alla sua lettera
I had to answer his/her letter straight away

devi lavorare di più
you must work harder

dovettero portare il loro bagaglio sull'aereo
they had to carry their luggage onto the plane

In the conditional, dovere can be used to give advice (present conditional) or to express what should have been done (past conditional):

dovresti mangiare più verdura
you should eat more vegetables

avrebbero dovuto evitare quell'incontro
they should have avoided that meeting

b) *Probability*

dev'essere ancora addormentata
she must be still asleep

la levata della posta dev'essere a mezzogiorno
the mail collection must be at midday

c) *Intention, expectation*

devo proprio andare ora
I really must go now

il treno deve arrivare alle otto
the train is due to arrive at eight

2 POTERE (*conjugation* p 198)

expresses:

❑ capacity, ability
❑ permission
❑ possibility

a) *Capacity, ability*

posso mostrartelo subito
I can show it to you straight away

può fare dodici vasche senza fermarsi
he/she can swim twelve lengths without stopping

le mia macchina poteva fare i 150 all'ora
my car could do 150kph

b) *Permission*

posso entrare?
may I come in?

va bene, puoi guardare i cartoni animati
all right then, you can watch the cartoons

c) *Possibility*

può succedere
it can happen

può essere già partito
he may already have left

Note the following points:

i) With verbs of perception (eg sentire to hear/feel, vedere to see) potere is often omitted:

si vedeva l'aurora boreale
you could see the Northern lights

ii) In the conditional potere can be used to express indignation:

potresti salutare quando esci!
you might/could say goodbye when you leave!

avrebbe potuto prestarci dei soldi!
he/she/you could have lent us some money!

Note also the following idiomatic uses of potere:

non ne posso più
I can't stand it any more

è una persona che può molto
he/she is a very powerful person

3 VOLERE (*conjugation* p 205)

expresses:

❏ desire
❏ wish
❏ intention

a) *Desire*

voglio andarmene di qua
I want to leave here

vuol ballare?
do you want to dance?

b) *Wish*

vorrei comprare una nuova macchina
I would like to buy a new car

avrei voluto prenderlo a calci
I would have liked to kick him

c) *Intention*

voleva passare la notte alla stazione
he/she intended to spend the night at the station

cosa vuoi fare da grande?
what do you want to be when you grow up?

Note the following points:

i) volere has some idiomatic uses:

vuol bene alla famiglia
he/she loves his/her family

ogni mattina sembra che voglia piovere
every morning it looks as if it might rain

ii) with ci (idiomatic):

quanto ci vuole da qui alla stazione?
how long does it take to get from here to the railway station?

ci vuole un bel coraggio　　**ci vogliono solo cinque minuti**
it takes some nerve　　it only takes five minutes

4 Other modal verbs

Other verbs can have a modal function (ie act as auxiliaries).
The most common are sapere (to know) and osare (to dare):

non oso disturbarlo　　**sai nuotare?**
I daren't disturb him　　can you swim?

> ## Note
>
> As a rule **sapere** means 'to know a fact', 'to know how to', while
> **conoscere** means 'to be acquainted with a person or place':
>
> **sa chi era Michelangelo?**
> do you know who Michelangelo was?
>
> **sai leggere i numeri romani?**
> can you read Roman numerals?
>
> **lei non sa chi sono io!**
> you don't know who you are talking to!
>
> **conoscevamo tutti a quel convegno**
> we knew everybody at that conference
>
> **lei non mi conosce**   **conosce un bravo idraulico?**
> you don't know me   do you know a good plumber?

5 Use of the auxiliary with modal verbs

As a rule the modal auxiliary verb takes the auxiliary of the verb it
precedes:

sono partito	→	**sono dovuto partire**
I've left		I had to leave
non ho dormito	→	**non ho potuto dormire**
I didn't sleep		I couldn't sleep

However, when the modal verb precedes an infinitive which takes
essere as its auxiliary, then the infinitive **avere** can also be used as
an alternative:

non sono potuto andare al mercato
non ho potuto andare al mercato
I couldn't go to the market

è voluto partire a tutti i costi
ha voluto partire a tutti i costi
he was determined to go at all costs

erano dovuti ritornare
avevano dovuto ritornare
they had to go back

For the agreement of past participles see **pp 174-5.**

6 Use of reflexives with modal verbs

When reflexive infinitives follow modal verbs, the reflexive
pronoun can either precede the modal verb or be joined to the
infinitive:

ti vuoi sbrigare?
vuoi sbrigarti?
will you hurry up!

si dovevano lavare con l'acqua fredda
dovevano lavarsi con l'acqua fredda
they had to wash in cold water

Note that in compound tenses, the modal verb takes **avere** as
its auxiliary when it precedes the reflexive infinitive. However, it
takes **essere** as its auxiliary when the reflexive pronoun precedes it:

Gabriele ha dovuto alzarsi presto
Gabriele si è dovuto alzare presto
Gabriele had to get up early

O CONJUGATION TABLES

The following verbs provide the main patterns of conjugation
including the conjugation of some common irregular verbs. They
are arranged in alphabetical order.

-are verb	*(see also* section A*)*	AMARE
-ere verb	*(see also* section A*)*	TEMERE
-ire verb	*(see also* section A*)*	SERVIRE
		FINIRE

Reflexive verb	*(see also* section D*)*	**LAVARSI**
Auxiliaries	*(see also* section C*)*	**AVERE**
		ESSERE
Modal Auxiliary Verbs	*(see also* p 180*)*	**DOVERE**
	(see also p 181*)*	**POTERE**
	(see also p 182*)*	**VOLERE**
Passive	*(see also* section M*)*	**ESSERE AMATO**
Common irregular verbs		**ANDARE**
		DARE
		DIRE
		FARE
		SAPERE
		STARE
		TENERE
		VENIRE

'**Chambers Italian Verbs**', a fully comprehensive list of Italian verbs and their conjugations, is also available in this series.

AMARE *to love*

PRESENT	IMPERFECT	FUTURE
1 amo	amavo	amerò
2 ami	amavi	amerai
3 ama	amava	amerà
1 amiamo	amavamo	ameremo
2 amate	amavate	amerete
3 amano	amavano	ameranno
PASSATO REMOTO	**PASSATO PROSSIMO**	**PLUPERFECT**
1 amai	ho amato	avevo amato
2 amasti	hai amato	avevi amato
3 amò	ha amato	aveva amato
1 amammo	abbiamo amato	avevamo amato
2 amaste	avete amato	avevate amato
3 amarono	hanno amato	avevano amato
PAST ANTERIOR		**FUTURE PERFECT**
ebbi amato *etc*		avrò amato *etc*

CONDITIONAL

IMPERATIVE

PRESENT	PAST	
1 amerei	avrei amato	
2 ameresti	avresti amato	ama
3 amerebbe	avrebbe amato	ami
1 ameremmo	avremmo amato	amiamo
2 amereste	avreste amato	amate
3 amerebbero	avrebbero amato	amino

SUBJUNCTIVE

PRESENT	IMPERFECT	PLUPERFECT
1 ami	amassi	avessi amato
2 ami	amassi	avessi amato
3 ami	amasse	avesse amato
1 amiamo	amassimo	avessimo amato
2 amiate	amaste	aveste amato
3 amino	amassero	avessero amato
PASSATO	abbia amato *etc*	

INFINITIVE	GERUND	PAST PARTICIPLE
PRESENT	amando	amato
amare		
PAST		
aver(e) amato		

ANDARE *to go*

PRESENT	IMPERFECT	FUTURE
1 vado	andavo	andrò
2 vai	andavi	andrai
3 va	andava	andrà
1 andiamo	andavamo	andremo
2 andate	andavate	andrete
3 vanno	andavano	andranno
PASSATO REMOTO	**PASSATO PROSSIMO**	**PLUPERFECT**
1 andai	sono andato/a	ero andato/a
2 andasti	sei andato/a	eri andato/a
3 andò	è andato/a	era andato/a
1 andammo	siamo andati/e	eravamo andati/e
2 andaste	siete andati/e	eravate andati/e
3 andarono	sono andati/e	erano andati/e
PAST ANTERIOR		**FUTURE PERFECT**
fui andato/a *etc*		sarò andato/a *etc*

CONDITIONAL		*IMPERATIVE*
PRESENT	**PAST**	
1 andrei	sarei andato/a	
2 andresti	saresti andato/a	va/vai/va'
3 andrebbe	sarebbe andato/a	vada
1 andremmo	saremmo andati/e	andiamo
2 andreste	sareste andati/e	andate
3 andrebbero	sarebbero andati/e	vadano

SUBJUNCTIVE		
PRESENT	**IMPERFECT**	**PLUPERFECT**
1 vada	andassi	fossi andato/a
2 vada	andassi	fossi andato/a
3 vada	andasse	fosse andato/a
1 andiamo	andassimo	fossimo andati/e
2 andiate	andaste	foste andati/e
3 vadano	andassero	fossero andati/e
PASSATO	sia andato/a *etc*	

INFINITIVE	*GERUND*	*PAST PARTICIPLE*
PRESENT	andando	andato/a/i/e
andare		
PAST		
esser(e) andato/a/i/e		

AVERE *to have*

PRESENT	IMPERFECT	FUTURE
1 ho	avevo	avrò
2 hai	avevi	avrai
3 ha	aveva	avrà
1 abbiamo	avevamo	avremo
2 avete	avevate	avrete
3 hanno	avevano	avranno
PASSATO REMOTO	**PASSATO PROSSIMO**	**PLUPERFECT**
1 ebbi	ho avuto	avevo avuto
2 avesti	hai avuto	avevi avuto
3 ebbe	ha avuto	aveva avuto
1 avemmo	abbiamo avuto	avevamo avuto
2 aveste	avete avuto	avevate avuto
3 ebbero	hanno avuto	avevano avuto
PAST ANTERIOR		**FUTURE PERFECT**
ebbi avuto *etc*		avrò avuto *etc*

CONDITIONAL

IMPERATIVE

PRESENT	PAST	
1 avrei	avrei avuto	
2 avresti	avresti avuto	abbi
3 avrebbe	avrebbe avuto	abbia
1 avremmo	avremmo avuto	abbiamo
2 avreste	avreste avuto	abbiate
3 avrebbero	avrebbero avuto	abbiano

SUBJUNCTIVE

PRESENT	IMPERFECT	PLUPERFECT
1 abbia	avessi	avessi avuto
2 abbia	avessi	avessi avuto
3 abbia	avesse	avesse avuto
1 abbiamo	avessimo	avessimo avuto
2 abbiate	aveste	aveste avuto
3 abbiano	avessero	avessero avuto
PASSATO	abbia avuto *etc*	

INFINITIVE

GERUND

PAST PARTICIPLE

PRESENT	avendo	avuto
avere		
PAST		
aver(e) avuto		

DARE *to give*

PRESENT	IMPERFECT	FUTURE
1 do	davo	darò
2 dai	davi	darai
3 dà	dava	darà
1 diamo	davamo	daremo
2 date	davate	darete
3 danno	davano	daranno
PASSATO REMOTO	**PASSATO PROSSIMO**	**PLUPERFECT**
1 diedi/detti	ho dato	avevo dato
2 desti	hai dato	avevi dato
3 diede/dette	ha dato	aveva dato
1 demmo	abbiamo dato	avevamo dato
2 deste	avete dato	avevate dato
3 diedero/dettero	hanno dato	avevano dato
PAST ANTERIOR		**FUTURE PERFECT**
ebbi dato *etc*		avrò dato *etc*

CONDITIONAL		*IMPERATIVE*
PRESENT	**PAST**	
1 darei	avrei dato	
2 daresti	avresti dato	dà/dai/da'
3 darebbe	avrebbe dato	dia
1 daremmo	avremmo dato	diamo
2 dareste	avreste dato	date
3 darebbero	avrebbero dato	diano

SUBJUNCTIVE		
PRESENT	**IMPERFECT**	**PLUPERFECT**
1 dia	dessi	avessi dato
2 dia	dessi	avessi dato
3 dia	desse	avesse dato
1 diamo	dessimo	avessimo dato
2 diate	deste	aveste dato
3 diano	dessero	avessero dato
PASSATO	abbia dato *etc*	

INFINITIVE	*GERUND*	*PAST PARTICIPLE*
PRESENT	dando	dato
dare		
PAST		
aver(e) dato		

DIRE *to say, tell*

PRESENT	IMPERFECT	FUTURE
1 dico	dicevo	dirò
2 dici	dicevi	dirai
3 dice	diceva	dirà
1 diciamo	dicevamo	diremo
2 dite	dicevate	direte
3 dicono	dicevano	diranno
PASSATO REMOTO	**PASSATO PROSSIMO**	**PLUPERFECT**
1 dissi	ho detto	avevo detto
2 dicesti	hai detto	avevi detto
3 disse	ha detto	aveva detto
1 dicemmo	abbiamo detto	avevamo detto
2 diceste	avete detto	avevate detto
3 dissero	hanno detto	avevano detto
PAST ANTERIOR		**FUTURE PERFECT**
ebbi detto *etc*		avrò detto *etc*

CONDITIONAL

IMPERATIVE

PRESENT	PAST	
1 direi	avrei detto	
2 diresti	avresti detto	di'
3 direbbe	avrebbe detto	dica
1 diremmo	avremmo detto	diciamo
2 direste	avreste detto	dite
3 direbbero	avrebbero detto	dicano

SUBJUNCTIVE

PRESENT	IMPERFECT	PLUPERFECT
1 dica	dicessi	avessi detto
2 dica	dicessi	avessi detto
3 dica	dicesse	avesse detto
1 diciamo	dicessimo	avessimo detto
2 diciate	diceste	aveste detto
3 dicano	dicessero	avessero detto
PASSATO	abbia detto *etc*	

INFINITIVE	GERUND	PAST PARTICIPLE
PRESENT	dicendo	detto
dire		
PAST		
aver(e) detto		

DOVERE *to have to, owe*

PRESENT	IMPERFECT	FUTURE
1 devo/debbo	dovevo	dovrò
2 devi	dovevi	dovrai
3 deve	doveva	dovrà
1 dobbiamo	dovevamo	dovremo
2 dovete	dovevate	dovrete
3 devono/debbono	dovevano	dovranno

PASSATO REMOTO	PASSATO PROSSIMO	PLUPERFECT
1 dovei/dovetti	ho dovuto	avevo dovuto
2 dovesti	hai dovuto	avevi dovuto
3 dové/dovette	ha dovuto	aveva dovuto
1 dovemmo	abbiamo dovuto	avevamo dovuto
2 doveste	avete dovuto	avevate dovuto
3 doverono/dovettero	hanno dovuto	avevano dovuto

PAST ANTERIOR		FUTURE PERFECT
ebbi dovuto *etc*		avrò dovuto *etc*

CONDITIONAL

PRESENT	PAST
1 dovrei	avrei dovuto
2 dovresti	avresti dovuto
3 dovrebbe	avrebbe dovuto
1 dovremmo	avremmo dovuto
2 dovreste	avreste dovuto
3 dovrebbero	avrebbero dovuto

SUBJUNCTIVE

PRESENT	IMPERFECT	PLUPERFECT
1 deva/debba	dovessi	avessi dovuto
2 deva/debba	dovessi	avessi dovuto
3 deva/debba	dovesse	avesse dovuto
1 dobbiamo	dovessimo	avessimo dovuto
2 dobbiate	doveste	aveste dovuto
3 devano/debbano	dovessero	avessero dovuto

PASSATO	abbia dovuto *etc*	

INFINITIVE	GERUND	PAST PARTICIPLE
	dovendo	dovuto
PRESENT		
dovere		
PAST		
aver(e) avuto		

Note that in compound tenses **dovere** takes the same auxiliary as the following verb, eg: I had to go = **sono dovuto/a andare**; I had to read = **ho dovuto leggere**

ESSERE *to be*

PRESENT	IMPERFECT	FUTURE
1 sono	ero	sarò
2 sei	eri	sarai
3 è	era	sarà
1 siamo	eravamo	saremo
2 siete	eravate	sarete
3 sono	erano	saranno

PASSATO REMOTO	PASSATO PROSSIMO	PLUPERFECT
1 fui	sono stato/a	ero stato/a
2 fosti	sei stato/a	eri stato/a
3 fu	è stato/a	era stato/a
1 fummo	siamo stati/e	eravamo stati/e
2 foste	siete stati/e	eravate stati/e
3 furono	sono stati/e	erano stati/e

PAST ANTERIOR		FUTURE PERFECT
fui stato/a *etc*		sarò stato/a *etc*

CONDITIONAL   IMPERATIVE

PRESENT	PAST	
1 sarei	sarei stato/a	
2 saresti	saresti stato/a	sii
3 sarebbe	sarebbe stato/a	sia
1 saremmo	saremmo stati/e	siamo
2 sareste	sareste stati/e	siate
3 sarebbero	sarebbero stati/e	siano

SUBJUNCTIVE

PRESENT	IMPERFECT	PLUPERFECT
1 sia	fossi	fossi stato/a
2 sia	fossi	fossi stato/a
3 sia	fosse	fosse stato/a
1 siamo	fossimo	fossimo stati/e
2 siate	foste	foste stati/e
3 siano	fossero	fossero stati/e
PASSATO	sia stato/a *etc*	

INFINITIVE   GERUND   PAST PARTICIPLE

PRESENT	essendo	stato/a/i/e
essere		

PAST
esser(e) stato/a/i/e

ESSERE AMATO *to be loved*

PRESENT	IMPERFECT	FUTURE
1 sono amato/a	ero amato/a	sarò amato/a
2 sei amato/a	eri amato/a	sarai amato/a
3 è amato/a	era amato/a	sarà amato/a
1 siamo amati/e	eravamo amati/e	saremo amati/e
2 siete amati/e	eravate amati/e	sarete amati/e
3 sono amati/e	erano amati/e	saranno amati/e

PASSATO REMOTO	PASSATO PROSSIMO	PLUPERFECT
1 fui amato/a	sono stato/a amato/a	ero stato/a amato/a
2 fosti amato/a	sei stato/a amato/a	eri stato/a amato/a
3 fu amato/a	è stato/a amato/a	era stato/a amato/a
1 fummo amati/e	siamo stati/e amati/e	eravamo stati/e amati/e
2 foste amati/e	siete stati/e amati/e	eravate stati/e amati/e
3 furono amati/e	sono stati/e amati/e	erano stati/e amati/e

PAST ANTERIOR		FUTURE PERFECT
fui stato/a amato/a *etc*		sarò stato/a amato/a *etc*

CONDITIONAL		IMPERATIVE

PRESENT	PAST
1 sarei amato/a	sarei stato/a amato/a
2 saresti amato/a	saresti stato/a amato/a
3 sarebbe amato/a	sarebbe stato/a amato/a
1 saremmo amati/e	saremmo stati/e amati/e
2 sareste amati/e	sareste stati/e amati/e
3 sarebbero amati/e	sarebbero stati/e amati/e

SUBJUNCTIVE

PRESENT	IMPERFECT	PLUPERFECT
1 sia amato/a	fossi amato/a	fossi stato/a amato/a
2 sia amato/a	fossi amato/a	fossi stato/a amato/a
3 sia amato/a	fosse amato/a	fosse stato/a amato/a
1 siamo amati/e	fossimo amati/e	fossimo stati/e amati/e
2 siate amati/e	foste amati/e	foste stati/e amati/e
3 siano amati/e	fossero amati/e	fossero stati/e amati/e

PASSATO		
sia stato/a amati/e *etc*		

INFINITIVE	GERUND	PAST PARTICIPLE
PRESENT	essendo amato/a/i/e	essendo stato/a/i/e
esser(e) amato/a/i/e		amato/a/i/e
PAST		
esser(e) stato/a/i/e amato/a/i/e		

FARE *to do, make*

PRESENT	IMPERFECT	FUTURE
1 faccio	facevo	farò
2 fai	facevi	farai
3 fa	faceva	farà
1 facciamo	facevamo	faremo
2 fate	facevate	farete
3 fanno	facevano	faranno
PASSATO REMOTO	**PASSATO PROSSIMO**	**PLUPERFECT**
1 feci	ho fatto	avevo fatto
2 facesti	hai fatto	avevi fatto
3 fece	ha fatto	aveva fatto
1 facemmo	abbiamo fatto	avevamo fatto
2 faceste	avete fatto	avevate fatto
3 fecero	hanno fatto	avevano fatto
PAST ANTERIOR		**FUTURE PERFECT**
ebbi fatto *etc*		avrò fatto *etc*

CONDITIONAL		IMPERATIVE
PRESENT	PAST	
1 farei	avrei fatto	
2 faresti	avresti fatto	fa/fai/fa'
3 farebbe	avrebbe fatto	faccia
1 faremmo	avremmo fatto	facciamo
2 fareste	avreste fatto	fate
3 farebbero	avrebbero fatto	facciano

SUBJUNCTIVE		
PRESENT	IMPERFECT	PLUPERFECT
1 faccia	facessi	avessi fatto
2 faccia	facessi	avessi fatto
3 faccia	facesse	avesse fatto
1 facciamo	facessimo	avessimo fatto
2 facciate	faceste	aveste fatto
3 facciano	facessero	avessero fatto
PASSATO	abbia fatto *etc*	

INFINITIVE	GERUND	PAST PARTICIPLE
PRESENT	facendo	fatto
fare		
PAST		
aver(e) fatto		

FINIRE *to finish, end*

PRESENT	IMPERFECT	FUTURE
1 finisco	finivo	finirò
2 finisci	finivi	finirai
3 finisce	finiva	finirà
1 finiamo	finivamo	finiremo
2 finite	finivate	finirete
3 finiscono	finivano	finiranno
PASSATO REMOTO	**PASSATO PROSSIMO**	**PLUPERFECT**
1 finii	ho finito	avevo finito
2 finisti	hai finito	avevi finito
3 finì	ha finito	aveva finito
1 finimmo	abbiamo finito	avevamo finito
2 finiste	avete finito	avevate finito
3 finirono	hanno finito	avevano finito
PAST ANTERIOR		**FUTURE PERFECT**
ebbi finito *etc*		avrò finito *etc*

CONDITIONAL		IMPERATIVE
PRESENT	PAST	
1 finirei	avrei finito	
2 finiresti	avresti finito	finisci
3 finirebbe	avrebbe finito	finisca
1 finiremmo	avremmo finito	finiamo
2 finireste	avreste finito	finite
3 finirebbero	avrebbero finito	finiscano

SUBJUNCTIVE		
PRESENT	IMPERFECT	PLUPERFECT
1 finisca	finissi	avessi finito
2 finisca	finissi	avessi finito
3 finisca	finisse	avesse finito
1 finiamo	finissimo	avessimo finito
2 finiate	finiste	aveste finito
3 finiscano	finissero	avessero finito
PASSATO	abbia finito *etc*	

INFINITIVE	GERUND	PAST PARTICIPLE
PRESENT	finendo	finito
finire		
PAST		
aver(e) finito		

LAVARSI *to have a wash*

PRESENT	IMPERFECT	FUTURE
1 mi lavo	mi lavavo	mi laverò
2 ti lavi	ti lavavi	ti laverai
3 si lava	si lavava	si laverà
1 ci laviamo	ci lavavamo	ci laveremo
2 vi lavate	vi lavavate	vi laverete
3 si lavano	si lavavano	si laveranno

PASSATO REMOTO	PASSATO PROSSIMO	PLUPERFECT
1 mi lavai	mi sono lavato/a	mi ero lavato/a
2 ti lavasti	ti sei lavato/a	ti eri lavato/a
3 si lavò	si è lavato/a	si era lavato/a
1 ci lavammo	ci siamo lavati/e	ci eravamo lavati/e
2 vi lavaste	vi siete lavati/e	vi eravate lavati/e
3 si lavarono	si sono lavati/e	si erano lavati/e

PAST ANTERIOR		FUTURE PERFECT
mi fui lavato/a *etc*		mi sarò lavato/a *etc*

CONDITIONAL   IMPERATIVE

PRESENT	PAST	
1 mi laverei	mi sarei lavato/a	
2 ti laveresti	ti saresti lavato/a	lavati
3 si laverebbe	si sarebbe lavato/a	si lavi
1 ci laveremmo	ci saremmo lavati/e	laviamoci
2 vi lavereste	vi sareste lavati/e	lavatevi
3 si laverebbero	si sarebbero lavati/e	si lavino

SUBJUNCTIVE

PRESENT	IMPERFECT	PLUPERFECT
1 mi lavi	mi lavassi	mi fossi lavato/a
2 ti lavi	ti lavassi	ti fossi lavato/a
3 si lavi	si lavasse	si fosse lavato/a
1 ci laviamo	ci lavassimo	ci fossimo lavati/e
2 vi laviate	vi lavaste	vi foste lavati/e
3 si lavino	si lavassero	si fossero lavati/e
PASSATO	mi sia lavato/a *etc*	

INFINITIVE	GERUND	PAST PARTICIPLE
PRESENT	lavandomi	lavato/a/i/e
lavarsi		
PAST		
essersi lavato/a/i/e		

POTERE *to be able to*

PRESENT	IMPERFECT	FUTURE
1 posso	potevo	potrò
2 puoi	potevi	potrai
3 può	poteva	potrà
1 possiamo	potevamo	potremo
2 potete	potevate	potrete
3 possono	potevano	potranno

PASSATO REMOTO	PASSATO PROSSIMO	PLUPERFECT
1 potei/potetti	ho potuto	avevo potuto
2 potesti	hai potuto	avevi potuto
3 poté/potette	ha potuto	aveva potuto
1 potemmo	abbiamo potuto	avevamo potuto
2 poteste	avete potuto	avevate potuto
3 poterono/potettero	hanno potuto	avevano potuto

PAST ANTERIOR		FUTURE PERFECT
ebbi potuto *etc*		avrò potuto *etc*

CONDITIONAL

PRESENT	PAST
1 potrei	avrei potuto
2 potresti	avresti potuto
3 potrebbe	avrebbe potuto
1 potremmo	avremmo potuto
2 potreste	avreste potuto
3 potrebbero	avrebbero potuto

IMPERATIVE

SUBJUNCTIVE

PRESENT	IMPERFECT	PLUPERFECT
1 possa	potessi	avessi potuto
2 possa	potessi	avessi potuto
3 possa	potesse	avesse potuto
1 possiamo	potessimo	avessimo potuto
2 possiate	poteste	aveste potuto
3 possano	potessero	avessero potuto
PASSATO	abbia potuto *etc*	

INFINITIVE

	GERUND	PAST PARTICIPLE
	potendo	potuto

PRESENT
potere
PAST
aver(e) potuto

Note that in compound tenses potere takes the same auxiliary as the following verb, eg: I was able to come = sono potuto/a venire; I was able to eat = ho potuto mangiare

SAPERE *to know, know how to*

PRESENT	IMPERFECT	FUTURE
1 so	sapevo	saprò
2 sai	sapevi	saprai
3 sa	sapeva	saprà
1 sappiamo	sapevamo	sapremo
2 sapete	sapevate	saprete
3 sanno	sapevano	sapranno
PASSATO REMOTO	**PASSATO PROSSIMO**	**PLUPERFECT**
1 seppi	ho saputo	avevo saputo
2 sapesti	hai saputo	avevi saputo
3 seppe	ha saputo	aveva saputo
1 sapemmo	abbiamo saputo	avevamo saputo
2 sapeste	avete saputo	avevate saputo
3 seppero	hanno saputo	avevano saputo
PAST ANTERIOR		**FUTURE PERFECT**
ebbi saputo *etc*		avrò saputo *etc*

CONDITIONAL

IMPERATIVE

PRESENT	PAST	
1 saprei	avrei saputo	
2 sapresti	avresti saputo	sappi
3 saprebbe	avrebbe saputo	sappia
1 sapremmo	avremmo saputo	sappiamo
2 sapreste	avreste saputo	sappiate
3 saprebbero	avrebbero saputo	sappiano

SUBJUNCTIVE

PRESENT	IMPERFECT	PLUPERFECT
1 sappia	sapessi	avessi saputo
2 sappia	sapessi	avessi saputo
3 sappia	sapesse	avesse saputo
1 sappiamo	sapessimo	avessimo saputo
2 sappiate	sapeste	aveste saputo
3 sappiano	sapessero	avessero saputo
PASSATO	abbia saputo *etc*	

INFINITIVE

GERUND

PAST PARTICIPLE

PRESENT	sapendo	saputo
sapere		
PAST		
aver(e) saputo		

SERVIRE *to serve*

PRESENT	IMPERFECT	FUTURE
1 servo	servivo	servirò
2 servi	servivi	servirai
3 serve	serviva	servirà
1 serviamo	servivamo	serviremo
2 servite	servivate	servirete
3 servono	servivano	serviranno
PASSATO REMOTO	**PASSATO PROSSIMO**	**PLUPERFECT**
1 servii	ho servito	avevo servito
2 servisti	hai servito	avevi servito
3 servì	ha servito	aveva servito
1 servimmo	abbiamo servito	avevamo servito
2 serviste	avete servito	avevate servito
3 servirono	hanno servito	avevano servito
PAST ANTERIOR		**FUTURE PERFECT**
ebbi servito *etc*		avrò servito *etc*

CONDITIONAL		IMPERATIVE
PRESENT	**PAST**	
1 servirei	avrei servito	
2 serviresti	avresti servito	servi
3 servirebbe	avrebbe servito	serva
1 serviremmo	avremmo servito	serviamo
2 servireste	avreste servito	servite
3 servirebbero	avrebbero servito	servano

SUBJUNCTIVE		
PRESENT	**IMPERFECT**	**PLUPERFECT**
1 serva	servissi	avessi servito
2 serva	servissi	avessi servito
3 serva	servisse	avesse servito
1 serviamo	servissimo	avessimo servito
2 serviate	serviste	aveste servito
3 servano	servissero	avessero servito
PASSATO	abbia servito *etc*	

INFINITIVE	GERUND	PAST PARTICIPLE
PRESENT	servendo	servito
servire		
PAST		
aver(e) servito		

STARE _to be_

PRESENT	IMPERFECT	FUTURE
1 sto	stavo	starò
2 stai	stavi	starai
3 sta	stava	starà
1 stiamo	stavamo	staremo
2 state	stavate	starete
3 stanno	stavano	staranno
PASSATO REMOTO	**PASSATO PROSSIMO**	**PLUPERFECT**
1 stetti	sono stato/a	ero stato/a
2 stesti	sei stato/a	eri stato/a
3 stette	è stato/a	era stato/a
1 stemmo	siamo stati/e	eravamo stati/e
2 steste	siete stati/e	eravate stati/e
3 stettero	sono stati/e	erano stati/e
PAST ANTERIOR		**FUTURE PERFECT**
fui stato/a _etc_		sarò stato/a _etc_

CONDITIONAL		_IMPERATIVE_
PRESENT	PAST	
1 starei	sarei stato/a	
2 staresti	saresti stato/a	sta/stai/sta'
3 starebbe	sarebbe stato/a	stia
1 staremmo	saremmo stati/e	stiamo
2 stareste	sareste stati/e	state
3 starebbero	sarebbero stati/e	stiano

SUBJUNCTIVE		
PRESENT	IMPERFECT	PLUPERFECT
1 stia	stessi	fossi stato/a
2 stia	stessi	fossi stato/a
3 stia	stesse	fosse stato/a
1 stiamo	stessimo	fossimo stati/e
2 stiate	steste	foste stati/e
3 stiano	stessero	fossero stati/e
PASSATO	sia stato/a _etc_	

INFINITIVE	_GERUND_	_PAST PARTICIPLE_
PRESENT	stando	stato/a/i/e
stare		
PAST		
esser(e) stato/a/i/e		

TEMERE *to fear, be afraid of*

PRESENT	IMPERFECT	FUTURE
1 temo	temevo	temerò
2 temi	temevi	temerai
3 teme	temeva	temerà
1 temiamo	temevamo	temeremo
2 temete	temevate	temerete
3 temono	temevano	temeranno
PASSATO REMOTO	**PASSATO PROSSIMO**	**PLUPERFECT**
1 temei/temetti	ho temuto	avevo temuto
2 temesti	hai temuto	avevi temuto
3 temé/temette	ha temuto	aveva temuto
1 tamemmo	abbiamo temuto	avevamo temuto
2 temeste	avete temuto	avevate temuto
3 temerono/temettero	hanno temuto	avevano temuto
PAST ANTERIOR		**FUTURE PERFECT**
ebbi temuto *etc*		avrò temuto *etc*

CONDITIONAL

IMPERATIVE

PRESENT	PAST	
1 temerei	avrei temuto	
2 temeresti	avresti temuto	temi
3 temerebbe	avrebbe temuto	tema
1 temeremmo	avremmo temuto	temiamo
2 temereste	avreste temuto	temete
3 temerebbero	avrebbero temuto	temano

SUBJUNCTIVE

PRESENT	IMPERFECT	PLUPERFECT
1 tema	temessi	avessi temuto
2 tema	temessi	avessi temuto
3 tema	temesse	avesse temuto
1 temiamo	temessimo	avessimo temuto
2 temiate	temeste	aveste temuto
3 temano	temessero	avessero temuto
PASSATO	abbia temuto *etc*	

INFINITIVE

GERUND

PAST PARTICIPLE

PRESENT	temendo	temuto
temere		
PAST		
aver(e) temuto		

TENERE *to hold*

PRESENT	IMPERFECT	FUTURE
1 tengo	tenevo	terrò
2 tieni	tenevi	terrai
3 tiene	teneva	terrà
1 teniamo	tenevamo	terremo
2 tenete	tenevate	terrete
3 tengono	tenevano	terranno
PASSATO REMOTO	**PASSATO PROSSIMO**	**PLUPERFECT**
1 tenni	ho tenuto	avevo tenuto
2 tenesti	hai tenuto	avevi tenuto
3 tenne	ha tenuto	aveva tenuto
1 tenemmo	abbiamo tenuto	avevamo tenuto
2 teneste	avete tenuto	avevate tenuto
3 tennero	hanno tenuto	avevano tenuto
PAST ANTERIOR		**FUTURE PERFECT**
ebbi tenuto *etc*		avrò tenuto *etc*

CONDITIONAL | IMPERATIVE

PRESENT	PAST	
1 terrei	avrei tenuto	
2 terresti	avresti tenuto	tieni
3 terrebbe	avrebbe tenuto	tenga
1 terremmo	avremmo tenuto	teniamo
2 terreste	avreste tenuto	tenete
3 terrebbero	avrebbero tenuto	tengano

SUBJUNCTIVE

PRESENT	IMPERFECT	PLUPERFECT
1 tenga	tenessi	avessi tenuto
2 tenga	tenessi	avessi tenuto
3 tenga	tenesse	avesse tenuto
1 teniamo	tenessimo	avessimo tenuto
2 teniate	teneste	aveste tenuto
3 tengano	tenessero	avessero tenuto
PASSATO	abbia tenuto *etc*	

INFINITIVE | GERUND | PAST PARTICIPLE

	GERUND	PAST PARTICIPLE
PRESENT	tenendo	tenuto
tenere		
PAST		
aver(e) tenuto		

VENIRE *to come*

PRESENT	IMPERFECT	FUTURE
1 vengo	venivo	verrò
2 vieni	venivi	verrai
3 viene	veniva	verrà
1 veniamo	venivamo	verremo
2 venite	venivate	verrete
3 vengono	venivano	verranno

PASSATO REMOTO	PASSATO PROSSIMO	PLUPERFECT
1 venni	sono venuto/a	ero venuto/a
2 venisti	sei venuto/a	eri venuto/a
3 venne	è venuto/a	era venuto/a
1 venimmo	siamo venuti/e	eravamo venuti/e
2 veniste	siete venuti/e	eravate venuti/e
3 vennero	sono venuti/e	erano venuti/e

PAST ANTERIOR		FUTURE PERFECT
fui venuto/a *etc*		sarò venuto/a *etc*

CONDITIONAL		*IMPERATIVE*

PRESENT	PAST	
1 verrei	sarei venuto/a	
2 verresti	saresti venuto/a	vieni
3 verrebbe	sarebbe venuto/a	venga
1 verremmo	saremmo venuti/e	veniamo
2 verreste	sareste venuti/e	venite
3 verrebbero	sarebbero venuti/e	vengano

SUBJUNCTIVE

PRESENT	IMPERFECT	PLUPERFECT
1 venga	venissi	fossi venuto/a
2 venga	venissi	fossi venuto/a
3 venga	venisse	fosse venuto/a
1 veniamo	venissimo	fossimo venuti/e
2 veniate	veniste	foste venuti/e
3 vengano	venissero	fossero venuti/e

PASSATO		
sia venuto/a *etc*		

INFINITIVE	*GERUND*	*PAST PARTICIPLE*
PRESENT	venendo	venuto/a/i/e
venire		
PAST		
esser(e) venuto/a/i/e		

VOLERE *to want*

PRESENT	IMPERFECT	FUTURE
1 voglio	volevo	vorrò
2 vuoi	volevi	vorrai
3 vuole	voleva	vorrà
1 vogliamo	volevamo	vorremo
2 volete	volevate	vorrete
3 vogliono	volevano	vorranno
PASSATO REMOTO	**PASSATO PROSSIMO**	**PLUPERFECT**
1 volli	ho voluto	avevo voluto
2 volesti	hai voluto	avevi voluto
3 volle	ha voluto	aveva voluto
1 volemmo	abbiamo voluto	avevamo voluto
2 voleste	avete voluto	avevate voluto
3 vollero	hanno voluto	avevano voluto
PAST ANTERIOR		**FUTURE PERFECT**
ebbi voluto *etc*		avrò voluto *etc*

CONDITIONAL

IMPERATIVE

PRESENT	PAST
1 vorrei	avrei voluto
2 vorresti	avresti voluto
3 vorrebbe	avrebbe voluto
1 vorremmo	avremmo voluto
2 vorreste	avreste voluto
3 vorrebbero	avrebbero voluto

SUBJUNCTIVE

PRESENT	IMPERFECT	PLUPERFECT
1 voglia	volessi	avessi voluto
2 voglia	volessi	avessi voluto
3 voglia	volesse	avesse voluto
1 vogliamo	volessimo	avessimo voluto
2 vogliate	voleste	aveste voluto
3 vogliano	volessero	avessero voluto
PASSATO	abbia voluto *etc*	

INFINITIVE

GERUND

PAST PARTICIPLE

PRESENT

volere

PAST

aver(e) voluto

GERUND

volendo

PAST PARTICIPLE

voluto

Note that in compound tenses as an auxiliary volere
takes the same auxiliary as the following verb,
eg: I wanted to eat = ho voluto mangiare; I wanted to
go = sono voluto/a andare

P VERBAL CONSTRUCTIONS

In Italian there are two main types of verbal construction. Verbs can be followed:

❏ by another verb in the infinitive
❏ by an object (a noun or a pronoun)

1 Verbs followed by an infinitive

There are four main constructions where a verb is followed by an infinitive:

❏ verb + infinitive (no linking preposition)
❏ verb + di + infinitive
❏ verb + a + infinitive
❏ verb + da + infinitive

For examples of these four types of construction, see **pp 164-8.**

*asterisked verbs also admit other constructions.

a) *Verbs followed by an infinitive without preposition*

adorare	to adore (doing)
amare	to love (doing, to do)
*bastare	to be enough (to do)
bisogna *(impers)*	to need (to do)
convenire	to be worthwhile (doing)
*desiderare	to want (to do), to wish (to do)
dovere	to have to (do)
fare	to make (do)
giovare	to be useful (to do)
importare	to be important (to do)
*lasciare	to let (do), to allow (to do)
occorrere	to be necessary (to do)
osare	to dare (to do)
*piacere	to like (doing, to do)

potere	to be able to (do)
preferire	to prefer (doing, to do)
sapere	to know how (to do)
*sembrare	to seem (to do)
sentire	to feel (doing), to hear (doing)
solere	to be used to (doing)
toccare	to be one's turn (to do)
udire	to hear (doing)
vedere	to see (doing)
volere	to want (to do)

mi piacerebbe vederti
I'd like to see you

tocca a te telefonargli
it's your turn to phone him/them

b) *Verbs followed by* di + *infinitive*

accettare di	to agree (to do)
accorgersi di	to notice (that), to realize (that)
accusare di	to accuse of (doing)
ammettere di	to admit to (doing)
*aspettare di	to wait (to do)
aspettarsi di	to expect (to do)
assicurare di	to assure (that)
augurare di	to wish (to do)
*badare di	to be careful (to do), to make sure (of doing)
capitare di	to happen (to do)
cercare di	to try (to do)
cessare di	to cease (doing), to stop (doing)
chiedere di	to ask (to do)
comandare di	to order (to do)
concedere di	to allow (to do)
consigliare di	to advise (to do)
contentarsi di	to content oneself with (doing)
credere di	to believe (that)
decidere di	to decide (to do)

dichiarare di	to declare (that)
dimenticare di	to forget (to do)
dimostrare di	to prove (that), to show (that)
dire di	to say (to do), to tell (to do)
*dispiacere di	to be sorry (to do)
dubitare di	to doubt (that)
escludere di	to exclude the possibility of (doing)
evitare di	to avoid (doing)
far conto di	to suppose (that)
figurarsi di	to imagine (that)
fingere di	to pretend (that)
finire di	to finish (doing)
giurare di	to swear (to do)
godere di	to enjoy (doing)
*guardare di	to take care (to do)
illudersi di	to delude oneself (that)
immaginarsi di	to think (that), to imagine (that)
impedire di	to prevent (from doing)
incaricare di	to ask (to do)
interessarsi di	to be interested in (doing)
mancare di	to fail (to do)
meravigliarsi di	to be amazed at (doing)
meritare di	to deserve (to do)
offrire di	to offer (to do)
ordinare di	to order (to do)
*parere di	to seem (to do)
parlare di	to talk (of doing)
pensare di	to think (of doing)
pentirsi di	to repent (of having done)
permettere di	to allow (to do)
*piacere di	to like (to do, doing)
pregare di	to pray (to do), to ask (to do)

preoccuparsi di	to worry about (doing), to trouble (to do)
pretendere di	to claim (to do)
proibire di	to forbid (to do)
promettere di	to promise (to do)
raccomandare di	to beg (to do), to exhort (to do)
rallegrarsi di	to be pleased (that)
ricordarsi di	to remember (to do/doing)
rifiutare di	to refuse (to do)
rincrescere di	to be sorry (to do)
scegliere di	to choose (to do)
scrivere di	to write (to do)
scusare di	to excuse (for doing)
*sembrare di	to seem (that)
*sentire di	to feel (that)
sforzarsi di	to try hard (to do)
smettere di	to stop (doing)
sognare di	to dream (of doing)
sopportare di	to put up (with doing)
sospettare di	to suspect (of doing)
sperare di	to hope (to do)
supplicare di	to beg (to do)
temere di	to fear (doing)
vantarsi di	to boast (that)
vergognarsi di	to be ashamed (of doing)
vietare di	to forbid (to do)

c) *Verbs followed by* a + *infinitive*

abituare a	to accustom (to doing)
abituarsi a	to get used (to doing)
accennare a	to make as if (to do), to look as if (one is doing)
accondiscendere a	to agree (to do)
acconsentire a	to consent (to do)

affrettarsi a	to rush (to do)
aiutare a	to help (to do)
andare a	to go (to do)
arrischiarsi a	to dare (to do)
arrivare a	to manage (to do)
*aspettare a	to wait (to do)
aspirare a	to have aspirations (to do)
*badare a	to mind (that)
cominciare a	to begin (to do)
concorrere a	to contribute (to doing)
condannare a	to condemn (to do)
consentire a	to consent (to do)
continuare a	to go on (doing)
contribuire a	to contribute (to doing)
convincere a	to persuade (to do)
costringere a	to compel (to do)
destinare a	to destine (to do)
divertirsi a	to enjoy (doing)
esercitarsi a	to practise (doing)
esitare a	to hesitate (to do)
giocare a	to play (at doing)
imparare a	to learn (to do)
impegnarsi a	to undertake (to do), to be engaged in (doing)
incitare a	to incite (to do)
indurre a	to induce (to do)
insegnare a	to teach (to do)
insistere a	to insist (on doing)
invitare a	to invite (to do)
mandare a	to send (to do)
mettersi a	to start (to do, doing)
obbligare a	to force (to do)
persuadere a	to persuade (to do)
prepararsi a	to get ready (to do)
provare a	to try (to do)

provvedere a	to see to (doing)
rassegnarsi a	to resign oneself (to doing)
rinunciare a	to give up (doing)
riprendere a	to start (to do) again
riuscire a	to succeed (in doing)
sbrigarsi a	to hurry up (and do)
servire a	to be useful (for doing)
spingere a	to urge (to do)
tardare a	to be late (in doing)
tenerci a	to be keen (on doing)
tornare a	to return (to doing), to go back (to doing)
venire a	to come (to do)

d) *Verbs followed by* da + *infinitive* (this construction is less common)

astenersi da	to abstain (from doing)
avere da	to have to (do)
contenersi da	to restrain oneself (from doing)
*diffidare da	to warn (against doing)
dissuadere da	to dissuade (from doing)
guardarsi da	to be careful of (doing), to beware of (doing)

Note the following common constructions:

fare da mangiare
to make something to eat

mi ha dato da mangiare
he/she gave me something to eat

lui paga da bere
he's buying the drinks

2 Verbs followed by an object

In general, verbs which take a direct object in Italian also take a direct object in English, and verbs which take an indirect object in Italian (ie verb + preposition + object) also take an indirect object in English. There are however some exceptions:

a) Some common verbs followed by an indirect object in English but not in Italian (the English preposition is not translated):

ascoltare	to listen to
aspettare	to wait for
attendere	to wait for
cercare	to look for
chiedere	to ask for
domandare	to ask for
far pagare	to charge for
guardare	to look at
pagare	to pay for

chiediamo il conto
let's ask for the bill

cercava le pantofole
he/she was looking for his/her slippers

b) Some verbs which take a direct object in English, but a + indirect object in Italian:

assomigliare a	to resemble
avvicinarsi a	to approach
concedere a	to allow
convenire a	to suit
credere a	to believe
disubbidire a	to disobey
far piacere a	to please
giocare a	to play *(game, sport)*
piacere a	to please
resistere a	to resist
rinunciare a	to give up
rispondere a	to answer
telefonare a	to phone
ubbidire a	to obey

telefoni all'editore
phone the publisher

credo a quello che dici
I believe what you say

vuoi giocare a scacchi?
do you want to play chess?

c) Verbs taking a direct object in English but di + indirect object in Italian:

accorgersi di	to notice
aver bisogno di	to need
diffidare/non fidarsi di	to mistrust
dubitare di	to doubt
fidarsi di	to trust
impadronirsi di	to seize
mancare di	to lack, to miss
ricordarsi di	to remember
servirsi di	to use

fidatevi della nostra esperienza
trust our experience

lui manca assolutamente di tatto
he is absolutely lacking in tact

mi sono sempre ricordato del tuo compleanno
I have always remembered your birthday

d) Some verbs take di or a before an object, whereas their English equivalent uses a different preposition:

i) verb + di + object:

incolpare di	to charge with
innamorarsi di	to fall in love with
meravigliarsi di	to wonder at
parlare di	to speak about
ridere di	to laugh at
riempire di	to fill with
ringraziare di	to thank for
trattarsi di	to be about, to be a question of
vivere di	to live on

non si tratta di soldi
it's not a question of money

vivevano di espedienti
they lived by their wits

riempirono i bicchieri di vino frizzante
they filled their glasses with sparkling wine

devo ringraziarvi della vostra cortesia
I must thank you for your kindness

ii) verb + a + object:

interessarsi a   to be interested in
pensare a   to think of/about

pensava solo alla sua moto
he/she only thought of his/her motorbike

e) Other constructions use different prepositions in English and Italian:

dipendere da   to depend on
parlare con   to speak to
entrare in   to enter

3 Verbs followed by one direct object and one indirect object

a) This is a very wide category of verbs. In general they are constructed in the same way as their English equivalents:

spiegare qualcosa a qualcuno
to explain something to somebody

ho venduto un pezzo di giardino ai vicini
I've sold a piece of my garden to my neighbours

Note that in this type of construction the preposition 'to' is often omitted in English, but a cannot be omitted in Italian. Particular care must be taken when object pronouns are used (*see* pp 78-80).

b) With verbs expressing the idea of 'taking away', a is translated by 'from' (qn = qualcuno, sb = somebody, qc = qualcosa and sth = something):

chiedere qc a qn	to ask sb for sth
domandare qc a qn	to ask sb for sth
levare qc a qn	to take sth away from sb
nascondere qc a qn	to hide sth from sb
portare via qc a qn	to take sth away from sb
prendere qc a qn	to take sth from sb
rubare qc a qn	to steal sth from sb
togliere qc a qn	to take sth away from sb

Alberto ci nascose la sua malattia
Alberto concealed his illness from us

non portargli via la palla
don't take his ball away from him

hanno rubato la valigia a mia madre
they have stolen my mother's suitcase

4 Verb + indirect object + di + infinitive

Some verbs which take a direct object in English are followed by a + object + di + infinitive in Italian (qn = qualcuno, sb = somebody, qc = qualcosa and sth = something):

chiedere a qn di fare qc	to ask sb to do sth
comandare a qn di fare qc	to order sb to do sth
consigliare a qn di fare qc	to advise sb to do sth
dire a qn di fare qc	to tell sb to do sth
domandare a qn di fare qc	to ask sb to do sth
ordinare a qn di fare qc	to order sb to do sth
permettere a qn di fare qc	to allow sb to do sth
proibire a qn di fare qc	to forbid sb to do sth
promettere a qn di fare qc	to promise sb to do sth
proporre a qn di fare qc	to offer to do sth for sb, to suggest to sb to do sth

chiedi alla segretaria di aiutarti
ask the secretary to help you

ordinò alla pattuglia di andare in perlustrazione
he ordered the patrol to go on reconnaissance

hanno promesso ai loro genitori di rientrare presto
they promised their parents that they would get home early

7 PREPOSITIONS

a) The following are prepositions which combine with the definite article to produce a single word (**preposizioni articolate**):

a	to	in	in
con	with	per	by, through
di	of	su	on
da	from, by		

Note that the combined forms with **per** will be found primarily in older written texts and are relatively rare in the modern spoken or written language; this is also true for the majority of the combined forms with **con**, only **col** and **coi** being still common:

	il	lo	l'	i	gli	la	l'	le
a	al	allo	all'	ai	agli	alla	all'	alle
di	del	dello	dell'	dei	degli	della	dell'	delle
da	dal	dallo	dall'	dai	dagli	dalla	dall'	dalle
in	nel	nello	nell'	nei	negli	nella	nell'	nelle
su	sul	sullo	sull'	sui	sugli	sulla	sull'	sulle

che cos'hai detto alla mamma?
what did you say to Mum?

la macchina dello zio
my uncle's car

è tornato ieri dagli Stati Uniti
he returned yesterday from the United States

ha cercato un libro sullo scaffale
he/she looked for a book on the shelf

c'è un po' d'insalata nel frigo
there's a little salad in the fridge

mangio l'insalata col/con il limone
I eat salad with lemon juice

b) The following prepositions usually take the preposition di before a pronoun:

contro*	against
dentro*	inside
dietro*	behind
dopo	after
fra/tra	among, between
presso*	near, c/o, almost
senza	without
sopra*	above, upon
sotto	under
su	on
verso	towards

contro di te
against you

dopo di lei
after her/you

dentro di me
inside me

su di esso
on it

senza di lui
without him

verso di loro
towards them

*The asterisked prepositions may also take a before a noun although in most cases this is less common:

dietro la casa/dietro alla casa
behind the house

il vescovado si trova dietro al duomo
the bishop's residence is behind the cathedral

dietro di lei c'è un posto libero
there's an empty seat behind you/her

presso il liceo c'è un'edicola
there's a newspaper kiosk near the school

a Roma abitava presso una famiglia
he/she used to live with a family in Rome

mia zia abita presso di noi
my aunt lives with us

Note that with fra/tra the preposition is sometimes omitted:

loro s'intendono molto bene fra (di) loro
they get along very well

fra me e te c'è stato un malinteso
there's been a misunderstanding between us

c) Prepositional phrases with a:

i)

accanto a	beside	incontro a	towards
addosso a	beside, right next to	innanzi a	before
circa a	regarding	insieme a	along with, together with
davanti a	in front of, before	intorno a	around
dinanzi a	in front of, before	quanto a	as for, as regards
dirimpetto a	opposite	riguardo a	regarding
fino/sino a	up to, until	rispetto a	regarding
		vicino a	near

mi sono seduta accanto a lui
I sat down next to him

c'è un lavasecco dirimpetto all'appartamento
there's a dry cleaner's opposite the flat

quanto a mio marito, può venire più tardi
as for my husband, he can come later on

abitano vicino a una centrale nucleare
they live near a nuclear power station

Note that dirimpetto also functions as an invariable adjective, in which case it must follow the noun:

i miei suoceri abitano nel palazzo dirimpetto
my parents-in-law live in the block of flats opposite

ii)

in cima a	at the top of, at the summit of
di faccia a	opposite, facing
in fondo a	at the bottom of
di fronte a	in front of, opposite, facing
in mezzo a	in the middle of
in testa a	at the head of

in cima alla montagna
at the top of the mountain

in fondo alla strada
at the bottom of the street

di fronte al duomo
in front of the cathedral

in mezzo alla pianura
in the middle of the plain

d) Prepositional phrases with di:

a causa di	because of, on account of
fuori di	out, outside
invece di	instead of
per mezzo di	by means of
prima di	before

il treno è bloccato a causa della neve
the train can't get through because of the snow

purtroppo Mario si è chiuso fuori di casa
unfortunately Mario locked himself out

ci è arrivato prima di me
he got there before I did

Note, however, the set expression:

fuori città
out of town

e) Prepositional phrases with da:

fin/sin da	(as) from, ever since
lontano da	far from
lungi da	far from

mi è piaciuto fin da bambina
I've liked it since I was a child

ha dovuto posteggiare lontano dal teatro
he/she had to park far away from the theatre

f) Other prepositions:

attraverso	across	mediante	by means of, through
durante	during	nonostante	in spite of
eccetto	except	salvo	except
fuorché	except	secondo	according to
malgrado	in spite of	tranne	except

attraverso il Tevere
across the Tiber

durante la tempesta
during the storm

malgrado i miei dubbi
in spite of my doubts

secondo me, è un errore
in my opinion, it's a mistake

g) Prepositional verbs:

These are not as common in Italian as they are in English. Some typical examples are:

buttare giù
to jot down

mettere su
to set up

buttai giù due righe
I jotted down a few lines

hanno messo su casa insieme
they've moved in together

For verbs requiring a preposition before a dependent infinitive, see pp 206-11, 215-6.

PREPOSITIONS

A (AD)

Note that **ad** may be substituted for **a** when the following word begins with a vowel (particularly the same vowel).

TO *(dative function)*	**l'ho regalato ad Angelo** I gave it to Angelo as a present
AT/TO *(place)*	**sono rimasto/andato a casa** I stayed at/went home
	hanno una casa al mare they have a house at the seaside
	andiamo al mare let's go to the seaside
	sono ancora a letto **è andato a letto tardi** I'm still in bed he went to bed late
	domani andremo a scuola we'll be going to school tomorrow

Note that **a** is always used with the names of towns or cities:

	abita a Pistoia he/she lives in Pistoia
	ogni tanto vado a Roma I go to Rome every so often
(with directions)	**a nord/a sud di Firenze** north/south of Florence
	voltai a destra/a sinistra I turned right/left
FROM *(distance)*	**a venti chilometri da Barga** twenty kilometres from Barga
	a pochi metri dall'incrocio a few metres from the crossroads
AT *(time)*	**a che ora parte? – alle due** what time are you leaving? – at two
	a Natale/Pasqua **a domani!** at Christmas/Easter see you tomorrow!

una volta al giorno/alla settimana
once a day/a week

(with adverbial phrases of time or quantity)

a poco a poco
little by little

a due a due
two by two

un poco alla volta
a little at a time

a centinaia/migliaia
by the hundreds/thousands

a volte
sometimes

a vita
for life

TO *(with certain adjectives)*

pronto a partire
ready to leave

disposto ad aiutare
willing to help

TO *(after ordinals, solo, unico)*

il primo ad andarsene
the first to leave

il solo a pagare
the only one to pay

(manner)

risotto alla milanese
risotto Milanese style

spaghetti al pomodoro
spaghetti with tomato sauce

carne alla griglia
grilled meat

tè al limone
tea with lemon

a bocca aperta
with one's mouth open

a mia insaputa
unbeknown to me

ad alta/a bassa voce
in a loud/low voice

imparare a memoria
to learn by heart

chiudere a chiave
to lock

dipinto a mano
hand-painted

(means of transport or method of operation)

andare a piedi
to go on foot

una barca a remi/a vela
a rowing/sailing boat

(invocation)

al fuoco!
fire!

al ladro!
stop thief!

(with games)	**giocare a tennis**	**giocare a scacchi**
	to play tennis	to play chess
(after many verbs)	*see pp 209–11*	

CON

WITH *(association)*	**vieni con me**
	come with me

IN; WITH *(manner)*	**con voce rauca**	
	in a hoarse voice	
	accettare con piacere	**procedere con calma**
	to accept with pleasure	to proceed calmly

WITH *(means)*	**con un coltello**	
	with a knife	
	fare di sì/di no con la testa	
	to nod/shake one's head	

(idioms)	**non possiamo andare con questa pioggia**	
	we can't go in this rain	
	e con questo?	**con mio gran dolore**
	so what?	to my great sorrow
	con mia grande sorpresa	
	to my great surprise	

DA

Note that *di* may be elided before a vowel but *da* never is.

FROM *(origin)*	**Leonardo da Vinci**
	lit. Leonardo from Vinci
	But: **sono di Bari**
	I'm from Bari
FROM *(motion)*	**da Pisa a Lucca**
	from Pisa to Lucca
	arrivo da Genova alle tre
	I'm arriving from Genoa at three

(manner)	**si è comportato da bambino** he behaved like a child

agire da pazzo
to act like a madman

vestirsi da pirata
to dress up as a pirate

da vicino/da lontano
close up/from a distance

andare da solo
to go by oneself

fare tutto da sé
to do everything oneself

TO/AT *(someone's home or workplace)*

vieni da me stasera
come to my house tonight

siamo andati dai Rossi
we went to the Rossis'

andare dal dentista/medico
to go to the dentist's/doctor's

andare dal parrucchiere
to go to the hairdresser's

(purpose)

una macchina da scrivere
a typewriter

uno spazzolino da denti
a toothbrush

un'asse da stiro
an ironing board

un costume da bagno
a swimming costume

la stanza da bagno
the bathroom

la camera da letto
the bedroom

il vino da tavola
table wine

una casa da affittare
a house to let

una tazza da caffè
a coffee cup

But: **una tazza di caffè**
a cup of coffee

(physical description)

la ragazza dai capelli rossi
the girl with red hair

il signore dall'aspetto elegante
the elegant-looking gentleman

(monetary value) **un biglietto da venti euro**
a twenty-euro note

un francobollo da quanto?
a stamp of what value?

FOR *(duration)* **abito a Roma da quattro anni**
I've been living in Rome for four years

lavoravo da sei mesi
I had been working for six months

For tenses with da *see* **p 144.**

(cause) **morire dal freddo**   **tremare dalla paura**
to die of cold   to shake with fear

TO *(before infinitive)* **niente da dire**   **molto da fare**
nothing to say   a lot to do

c'è un freddo da morire
it's freezing cold

pazzo da legare   **il prezzo da pagare**
mad as a hatter   the price to be paid

un problema da risolvere
a problem to solve

(idioms) **è un uomo da poco**
he's a worthless sort of man

da giovane mi piaceva ballare
when I was young I liked dancing

da piccolo/da vecchio
as a child/as an old man

da una parte ... dall'altra
on the one hand ... on the other hand

da parte mia
on my behalf

BY *(passive)*	**la cena è stata offerta da mio cognato** the dinner was paid for by my brother-in-law	

DI

Note that if followed by a vowel di becomes d'.

(genitive – belonging to)	**il canarino del nonno** granddad's canary	**il sistema dei trasporti** the transport system
	il presidente della repubblica the President of the republic	
OF *(specification)*	**l'isola d'Elba** the island of Elba	**la città di Modena** the city of Modena
SOME *(in partitives)*	**ho comprato delle albicocche** I bought some apricots	
	ci vuole un po' di sale it needs a little salt	
FROM *(origin)*	**sono di Ascoli Piceno** I'm from Ascoli Piceno	**un vino della Toscana** a wine from Tuscany
FROM *(motion)*	**è già partito di casa** he has already left home	
OF *(number or quantity)*	**un paio di scarpe** a pair of shoes	**un chilo di patate** a kilo of potatoes
	venti litri di benzina twenty litres of petrol	**un milione d'abitanti** one million inhabitants
IN *(time)*	**sono le sei di mattina** it's six in the morning	**di giorno/di notte** by day/by night
	di mattina/di sera in the morning/in the evening	
	d'estate/d'inverno in the summer/in the winter	
(with ages)	**un bambino di due anni** a two-year-old child	

	una donna d'una certa età	
	a middle-aged woman	
(composition or contents)	una camicetta di seta	
	a silk blouse	
	un vestito di lana	una catena d'oro
	a woollen dress	a gold chain
	una bottiglia di vino	un bicchiere d'acqua
	a bottle of wine	a glass of water
(manner)	di malavoglia	di nascosto
	unwillingly	furtively
	essere di malumore/di buonumore	
	to be ill-humoured/good-humoured	
	è andata via di corsa	
	she ran off	
(after certain adjectives)	è contento di rimanere a casa	
	he is happy to stay at home	
	sono degni di rispetto	
	they are worthy of respect	
	quell'armadio è pieno di roba	
	that cupboard is full of stuff	
	era vestita di nero	
	she was dressed in black	
(cause)	morire di fame	piangere di gioia
	to die of hunger	to weep with joy

For verbs which take di before a dependent infinitive see pp 207-9

THAN *(with comparatives before nouns, pronouns and numerals)*	hai viaggiato più di Stefano
	you've travelled more than Stefano
	hai letto più di me
	you've read more than me

	meno di cinque persone fewer than five people	
IN THE *(after superlatives)*	**il calciatore più famoso del mondo** the most famous footballer in the world	

(idioms)

cosa c'è di nuovo? what's new?	**niente di grave** nothing serious
lo conosco di vista I know him by sight	**dire di sì/di no** to say yes/no

dare del tu/del lei a qualcuno
to use the "tu"/the"lei" form with someone

IN

TO/IN   **essere/andare in cucina**
to be in/go to the kitchen

essere/andare in ufficio
to be in/go to the office

abitare/andare in centro
to live in/go to the town centre

avere una casa in campagna
to have a house in the country

Note that in is used with regions, countries, large islands and continents:

in Liguria ci sono molte stazioni balneari
in Liguria there are many holiday resorts

Treviso è nel Veneto
Treviso is in the Veneto

siamo in Francia/negli Stati Uniti per affari
we are in France/in the States on business

in Sardegna d'estate ci sono molti turisti
in Sardinia in the summer there are a lot of
tourists

la sua famiglia è emigrata in Australia
his/her family emigrated to Australia

IN *(expressions of time)* **in primavera/in autunno**
in the spring/in the autumn

gli Italiani vanno in ferie in agosto
Italians go on holiday in August

nel 1945 è finita la guerra
the war ended in 1945

viviamo nel Duemila
we are living in the twenty-first century

il treno è arrivato in orario/in ritardo
the train arrived on time/late

BY *(modes of transport)* **viaggiare in aereo/in treno/in pullman**
to travel by air/by train/by bus

andare in bicicletta
to cycle

IN *(manner)* **vivere in miseria**   **studiare in pace**
to live in poverty   to study in peace

ascoltare in silenzio   **è partito in fretta**
to listen in silence   he left in a hurry

fatto in casa
home-made

(idioms) **credere in Dio**   **eravamo in sette**
to believe in God   there were seven of us

parlare in italiano/in inglese
to speak in Italian/in English

è molto bravo nelle lingue ma non in matematica
he's very good at languages but not at maths

questa rivista è stata offerta in omaggio
this magazine was a free gift

stare in piedi   **balzai in piedi**
to stand   I leapt to my feet

PER

FOR *(intended for)*	**questo pacco è per te** this parcel is for you
FOR *(duration)*	**siamo qui per alcuni giorni** we are here for a few days
	sono rimasta a Venezia per una settimana I stayed in Venice for a week
FOR *(destination)*	**sono partiti per Torino** they left for Turin
(purpose)	**la crema per scarpe** shoe polish
	sono venuto per ringraziarti I've come to thank you
BY *(means)*	**viaggiare per terra/per mare** to travel by land/by sea
	mandare una lettera per via aerea to send a letter by airmail
	chiamare per telefono to phone
(place)	**vagava per le strade** he/she was wandering through the streets
	l'ho incontrato per strada I met him in the street
	l'hanno trovato disteso per terra they found him lying on the ground
	buttalo per terra throw it on the ground
	correre su/giù per la strada/le scale to run up/down the street/the stairs
	per di qua! **per di là!** this way! that way

ABOUT TO *(with* stare)	**stavano per pagare** they were about to pay	
(idioms)	**per favore/per piacere/per cortesia** please	
	per fortuna fortunately	**per caso** by chance
	per modo di dire so to speak	

SU

ON *(place)*	**sul tavolo c'era una bottiglia** on the table there was a bottle
	il cane era sdraiato sul tappeto the dog was stretched out on the carpet
ONTO *(literally and figuratively)*	**il gatto è saltato sul muro** the cat jumped onto the wall
	la casa dà sul mare the house looks out onto the sea
ON, ABOUT *(subject)*	**fece una conferenza sulla UE** he/she gave a lecture about the EU
ABOUT, AROUND *(approximation)*	**è un uomo sulla cinquantina** he's a man of about fifty
	la valigia sarà sui venti chili the case must weigh about twenty kilos
OUT OF *(fraction)*	**nove volte su dieci** nine times out of ten
(idioms)	**non mi hai mai preso sul serio** you have never taken me seriously
	l'ho letto sul giornale I read it in the newspaper

8 CONJUNCTIONS

Conjunctions are invariable parts of speech which link words, phrases or clauses. They can consist of one word or several words (conjunctive phrases).

e	o	ma
and	or	but
con tutto ciò	**anche se**	**di modo che**
in spite of it all	even though	so that

A COORDINATING CONJUNCTIONS

1 Definition

Coordinating conjunctions link two similar words or groups of words. The following are the principal coordinating conjunctions (or adverbs used as conjunctions):

e	anche	pure
and	also	also
né	neanche	nemmeno
nor	not even	not even
o	oppure	altrimenti
or	or, otherwise	otherwise, or else
ma	tuttavia	però
but	yet, however, nevertheless	but, yet, however, nevertheless
infatti	cioè	ossia
as a matter of fact, actually	that is, namely	that is, or rather
dunque	perciò	pertanto
so, therefore	so, therefore	so, therefore
quindi	ebbene	allora
so, therefore	well (then)	then

aveva fame e sete
he/she was hungry and thirsty

prendere o lasciare
take it or leave it

se avrò tempo andrò a piedi, altrimenti in bicicletta
if I have time I'll walk, otherwise I'll go on my bike

aveva poco tempo per cucinare, perciò comprò un forno a micro-onde
he/she had little time to cook, so he/she bought a microwave

Note

- When the conjunction **e** is placed in front of another vowel – **e** in particular – it is often changed to **ed**:

  è intelligente ed equilibrata   **il pane e(d) il vino**
  she's intelligent and well-balanced   bread and wine

- When **ma** is used to connect two clauses, a comma or a semicolon is always placed before it. When it joins two words or phrases in the same clause, no comma is added:

  uscì di casa, ma non andò a lavorare
  he/she left home but did not go to work

  uno scolaro intelligente ma pigro
  an intelligent but lazy schoolboy

---

2 Correlative conjunctions

e ... e and ... and	**ora ... ora** sometimes ... sometimes
o ... o either ... or	**né ... né** neither ... nor
non solo ... ma anche not only ... but also	**tanto ... quanto** as ... as

non c'era nessuno né alla fermata dell'autobus né al posteggio dei taxi
there was no one either at the bus stop or at the taxi rank

non solo si mise a piovere ma cominciò anche a grandinare
not only did it begin to rain, but it also began to hail

ora ride, ora piange
sometimes he/she smiles, sometimes he/she cries

B SUBORDINATING CONJUNCTIONS

1 Definition

These introduce a clause that cannot stand on its own as a full sentence but is dependent on another one, usually a main clause.

al punto che	dove
so much that	where
a patto che/a condizione che	finché
on condition that	until
appena	fin tanto che
as soon as	as long as
che (non)	giacché
that	as, since
come	in modo che
how, like, as soon as	so that, in such a way that
come se	mentre
as if	while, whereas
comunque	nel senso che
however	in the sense that
dal momento che	ogni volta che
since	every time that
dato che	perché
given that	why, because
dopo che	per quanto
after	although, even though
poiché	quantunque
as, since	although
prima che	se
before	if
purché	senza che
provided that	without

qualora	siccome
in case	as, since, because
quando	tanto ... che
when	so ... that

era tanto stanco che non riuscì a chiudere occhio
he was so tired that he couldn't sleep at all

siccome una lettera non sarebbe arrivata in tempo mandarono un fax
since a letter would not have arrived in time they sent a fax

voglio vedere dei miglioramenti prima che finisca il trimestre
I want to see some improvement before the term is over

la salutò come se la conoscesse
he/she greeted her as if he/she knew her

2 Conjunctions which are almost always used with the subjunctive

perché	affinché	che
so that	so that	so that
benché	sebbene	per quanto
(al)though	(al)though	although
nonostante che	purché	
even though, in spite of	provided that	

parla ad alta voce affinché tutti sentano
speak loudly so that everyone can hear

sebbene sia passato tanto tempo continua a parlarne
although so much time has gone by he/she keeps on talking about it

3 Correlative conjunctions

più ... che	meno ... che
more ... than	less ... than
più ... di quanto	meglio/peggio ... che
more ... than	better/worse ... than

la lavastoviglie consuma più elettricità di quanto non immaginassi
the dishwasher uses more electricity than I imagined

C CONJUNCTIONS WITH MORE THAN ONE MEANING

1 PERCHÉ

a) When perché means 'because' or 'why', it is followed by the indicative:

perché non hai preso l'ombrello? – perché faceva bel tempo quando sono uscito
why didn't you take your umbrella? – because when I went out the weather was fine

ieri non si alzò perché non si sentiva bene
yesterday he/she did not get up because he/she was not feeling well

b) When perché means 'so that', it is followed by the subjunctive:

ti telefono perché tu sappia quello che sta succedendo
I'm phoning so that you know what's happening

2 SE

a) When se introduces an if clause, it is followed either by the subjunctive or by the indicative (*see* p 158):

se mangiasse di meno non ingrasserebbe tanto
if he/she ate less, he/she wouldn't put on so much weight

perderai il treno se non corri
you'll miss the train if you don't run

b) When se expresses doubt, it is followed by the conditional or by the infinitive:

mi chiedo se accetterebbe questa proposta
I wonder if he/she would accept this proposal

non sapeva se ridere o piangere
he/she didn't know whether to laugh or cry

3 CHE

a) When che means 'that', it can be followed by the subjunctive or the indicative (*see also* p 144):

disse che lo aveva visto
he/she said that he/she had seen him

penso che tu abbia ragione
I think that you're right

non è prudente che vi mettiate in viaggio ora
it is not wise that you begin your journey now

spero che vi divertiate
I hope that you enjoy yourselves

b) When che means 'so that', it is followed by the subjunctive:

spiegai chiaramente la regola, che tutti potessero capire
I explained the rule clearly, so that everyone could understand

Note that some conjunctions such as dove, come, quando and perché could also be adverbs:

quando parti?	**telefonami quando arrivi**
when are you leaving? *(adverb)*	call me when you arrive *(conjunction)*

9 NUMBERS AND QUANTITY

A CARDINAL NUMBERS

0	zero	27	ventisette
1	uno	28	ventotto
2	due	29	ventinove
3	tre	30	trenta
4	quattro	40	quaranta
5	cinque	50	cinquanta
6	sei	60	sessanta
7	sette	70	settanta
8	otto	80	ottanta
9	nove	90	novanta
10	dieci	100	cento
11	undici	101	centouno
12	dodici	200	duecento
13	tredici	300	trecento
14	quattordici	400	quattrocento
15	quindici	500	cinquecento
16	sedici	600	seicento
17	diciassette	700	settecento
18	diciotto	800	ottocento
19	diciannove	900	novecento
20	venti	1000	mille
21	ventuno	1992	millenovecento
22	ventidue		novantadue
23	ventitré	2,000	duemila
24	ventiquattro	2,001	duemileuno
25	venticinque	5,000	cinquemila
26	ventisei	10,000	diecimila
		100,000	centomila

un milione, due milioni
one million, two million

un miliardo, due miliardi
one billion, two billion

Note the following points:

a) 'One' used on its own has two forms: uno *(masc)* and una *(fem)*:

ne voglio uno/una
I want one

'One' used in front of a noun behaves like an indefinite article and takes endings (un, uno, una, un'):

un libro	**uno studente**
one/a book	one/a student
una sterlina	**un'isola**
one/a pound	one/an island

b) The tens from venti to novanta lose their final vowel in front of uno and otto:

venti, ventuno, ventotto
twenty, twenty-one, twenty-eight

c) cento and mille are never preceded by one as in English. When preceded by other numbers, cento remains invariable:

trecento
three hundred

whilst mille changes to mila:

duemila
two thousand

d) Compounds with uno lose their final -o in front of a noun:

ventun ragazzi
twenty-one boys

e) Compounds ending with -tré always have an acute accent:

ventitré
twenty-three

f) milione and miliardo have plural forms and are always followed by **di** when used with a noun:

tre milioni di persone
three million people

g) Full stops and not commas are used to separate thousands (diecimila is written 10.000) and commas, not full stops, are used for decimals:

uno virgola sei (1,6)
one point six (1.6)

h) All numbers, single or compound, are written as one word but e (and) is often used to join hundreds to units or tens and to join thousands to units/tens/hundreds:

cento e uno	**duecento e tre**	**mille e due**
a hundred and one	two hundred and three	a thousand and two

tremila e sessanta	**diecimila e cinquecento**
three thousand and sixty	ten thousand five hundred

i) Numbers from 200 to 900 are used to express centuries as follows:

il Duecento	**il Trecento**	**il Quattrocento**
the 13th century	the 14th century	the 15th century
il Cinquecento	**il Seicento**	**il Settecento**
the 16th century	the 17th century	the 18th century
l'Ottocento	**il Novecento**	**il Duemila**
the 19th century	the 20th century	the 21st century

It is also possible to use Roman numerals:

nel XIX (diciannovesimo) secolo
in the 19th century

j) Approximate numbers:

una decina	**una dozzina**	**una quindicina**
about ten	about twelve	about fifteen
una ventina	**una trentina**	**un centinaio**
about twenty	about thirty	about a hundred
due centinaia	**un migliaio**	**due migliaia**
about two hundred	about a thousand	about two thousand

Note that di is used when approximate numbers are followed by a noun:

una decina di giorni	**un centinaio di persone**
about ten days	about a hundred people

Note the following idiomatic expressions:

vado a fare due/quattro passi	**dille tutto in due parole**
I'm going for a short walk	tell her everything in a few words

B ORDINAL NUMBERS

		abbreviations
1st	**primo, prima, primi, prime**	1°, 1ª, 1ⁱ, 1ᵉ
2nd	**secondo,** *etc*	2°, 2ª, 2ⁱ, 2ᵉ
3rd	**terzo**	3° *etc.*
4th	**quarto**	4°
5th	**quinto**	5°
6th	**sesto**	6°
7th	**settimo**	7°
8th	**ottavo**	8°
9th	**nono**	9°
10th	**decimo**	10°
11th	**undicesimo**	11°
12th	**dodicesimo**	12°
13th	**tredicesimo**	13°
14th	**quattordicesimo**	14°
15th	**quindicesimo**	15°
16th	**sedicesimo**	16°
17th	**diciassettesimo**	17°
18th	**diciottesimo**	18°

19th	diciannovesimo	19°
20th	ventesimo	20°
21st	ventunesimo	21°
22nd	ventiduesimo	22°
23rd	ventitreesimo	23°
28th	ventottesimo	28°
29th	ventinovesimo	29°
30th	trentesimo	30°
100th	centesimo	100°
101st	centounesimo	101°
200th	duecentesimo	200°
1,000th	millesimo	1.000°
10,000th	decimillesimo	10.000°

Note the following points:

a) Ordinal numbers after decimo are formed by adding -esimo to the cardinal number which drops its final vowel except in the case of tre and numbers ending in -tré.

b) Ordinal numbers belong to the class of adjectives ending in -o/a/i/e. These agree with the noun in gender and number and usually precede it except with names of popes and kings:

il quarto giorno
the fourth day

la quinta classe
the fifth class

i primi uomini
the first men

le prime file
the first rows

papa Paolo Sesto
Pope Paul VI

re Carlo Ottavo
King Charles VIII

c) Other special ordinal numbers are:

ennesimo/a/i/e
umpteenth, nth

ultimo/a/i/e
last

C MATHEMATICAL EXPRESSIONS

1 Vulgar fractions

Vulgar fractions are expressed as in English: cardinal number followed by ordinal number:

due quinti
two fifths

tre quarti
three quarters

un quinto
a fifth

un terzo
a third

mezzo
a half

Note that the article is omitted in Italian with mezzo:

quattro e mezzo
four and a half

2 Decimals

The English decimal point is conveyed by a comma in Italian (*see also* p 241):

tre virgola cinque (3,5)
three point five (3.5)

quattro virgola cinquantasei (4,56)
four point five six (4.56)

3 Percentages

Percentages are expressed as in English:

due per cento (2%)
two per cent (2%)

Note that Italian uses the definite article with percentages:

c'è stato un incremento del 2%
there has been a 2% increase

4 Arithmetic

Addition	**dieci più sei**	10+6
Subtraction	**otto meno tre**	8−3
Multiplication	**sette per due** *or* **sette volte due**	7×2
Division	**quattro diviso due**	4÷2
Square	**due al quadrato**	2^2
Square root	**la radice quadrata di quattro**	$\sqrt{4}$

D MEASUREMENTS AND PRICES

1 Measurements

a) *Dimensions and weight*

Mario è alto un metro e settanta e pesa settanta chili
Mario is one metre seventy tall and weighs seventy kilos

la classe è lunga 12 metri/è 12 metri di lunghezza
the classroom is 12 metres long

la classe è larga 8 metri/è 8 metri di larghezza
the classroom is 8 metres wide

il libro è spesso 5 centimetri/è 5 centimetri di spessore
the book is 5 centimetres thick

la mia camera misura 4 metri per 5
my bedroom is 4 metres by 5

b) *Distance*

quanto dista il centro? – circa tre chilometri
how far is the centre? – it's about three kilometres

ci troviamo a cinque chilometri dal mare
we are five kilometres from the sea

è lontana la stazione ferroviaria?
is the railway station far from here?

2 Prices

quanto costa/viene il vino alla bottiglia?
how much is a bottle of wine?

quanto costano/vengono le mele al chilo?
how much is a kilo of apples?

qual è il prezzo di una camera singola?
what is the price of a single room?

costa/viene 10 euro alla bottiglia it's 10 euros a bottle	**le mele sono a 3 euro al chilo** apples are 3 euros a kilo
quanto fa/quant'è in tutto? how much is it altogether?	**sono 4 euro in tutto** that comes to 4 euros altogether

 E EXPRESSIONS OF QUANTITY

Quantity may be expressed by an adverb, an adjective or a pronoun of quantity such as molto, troppo or by a noun which names the actual quantity involved, such as a bottle, a dozen.

1 Adverbs, adjectives and pronouns of quantity

quanto/a/i/e how much, how many	parecchio/parecchia/parecchi/parecchie quite a lot, several
molto/a/i/e much, many, a lot (of)	un mucchio (di) much, many, a lot (of)
poco/poca/pochi/poche little, few	un po' (di) some, a little
troppo/a/i/e too much, too many	troppo poco/poca/pochi/poche too little, too few
tanto/a/i/e so much, so many	tanto/a/i/e ... quanto/a/i/e ... as much/many ... as ...
meno less, fewer	più more
la maggior parte (di) most, the majority (of)	abbastanza enough

non ho molto tempo I haven't got much time	**ho parecchio lavoro** I have quite a lot of work
vorrei un po' di zucchero I'd like some sugar	**pochi sono venuti** few came
hanno tanti problemi they have a lot of problems	**quante valigie ti porti?** how many cases are you taking?
abbiamo più esperienza we have more experience	**oggi ci sono meno treni** today there are fewer trains
avete abbastanza soldi? have you got enough money?	**la maggior parte della gente** most people

2 Nouns expressing quantity + di + noun

un chilo di a kilo of	**una libbra di** a pound of	**un litro di** a litre of
un pezzo di a piece of	**una fetta di** a slice of	**una porzione di** a portion of
una scatola di a tin/box of	**una bottiglia di** a bottle of	**un vasetto di** a jar of
un pacchetto di a packet of	**una tazza di** a cup of	**un bicchiere di** a glass of
un cucchiaio di a spoonful of	**un boccone di** a mouthful of *(food)*	**un sorso di** a mouthful of *(drink)*
un paio di a pair of, a couple of		

vorrei una scatola di pomodori e un litro d'olio
I would like a tin of tomatoes and a litre of oil

ci vogliono un chilo e mezzo di farina e un paio d'uova
you need a kilo and a half of flour and a couple of eggs

3 Expressions of quantity used without a noun

When an expression of quantity is used without a noun, **di** is replaced by **ne** which goes in front of the verb (*see* pp 84-6):

abbiamo visitato molti musei; ne abbiamo visitati molti a Firenze
we visited a lot of museums; we visited a lot (of them) in Florence

10 EXPRESSIONS OF TIME

A THE TIME

che ora è, che ore sono?
what time is it?

The word ora/ore is only used in questions. The reply is:

sono + le + number

For example:

a) *Full hours*

	sono le due	**sono le undici**
	it's 2 o'clock	it's 11 o'clock
But:	**è l'una**	**è mezzogiorno/mezzanotte**
	it's 1 o'clock	it's midday/midnight

b) *Half-hours*

sono le cinque e mezzo/mezza	**è l'una e mezzo/mezza**
it's half past five	it's half past one
But:	**è la mezza**
	it's half past twelve

c) *Quarter-hours*

sono le nove e un quarto
it's quarter past nine

sono le nove meno un quarto
sono le otto e tre quarti
it's quarter to nine

d) *Minutes*

sono le sei e venti
it's twenty past six

sono le due meno cinque
it's five to two

Note that the word minuti is generally omitted.

e) *a.m. and p.m.*

There is no direct equivalent for these terms. Italian may use 'in the morning' or 'in the evening' as appropriate:

di mattina, del mattino in the morning (a.m.)	**di/del pomeriggio** in the afternoon (p.m.)
di sera in the evening (p.m.)	**di notte** at night (a.m.)
sono le sette del mattino it's seven a.m.	**sono le sei del pomeriggio** it's six p.m.
sono le dieci di sera it's ten p.m.	**sono le due di notte** it's two a.m.

f) *The 24-hour clock is normally used for timetables, time signals and so on:*

il treno delle tredici e quindici
the 13.15 train

ore venti e trentacinque minuti
the time is 8.35 p.m.

g) *At what time?, at ..., at about ..., from ... to ...*

a che ora parte l'aereo?
what time does the plane leave?

parte alle otto e cinque
it leaves at five past eight

quanto dura il viaggio?
how long does the journey take?

dura due ore
it takes two hours

quando vedi la tua amica?
when will you be seeing your friend?

la vedo verso le quattro
I'll be seeing her at about four

lavoro dalle nove alle cinque
I work from nine to five

B DATE AND AGE

1 Names of months, days and seasons

a) *Months* (i mesi)

gennaio	January
febbraio	February
marzo	March

aprile	April
maggio	May
giugno	June
luglio	July
agosto	August
settembre	September
ottobre	October
novembre	November
dicembre	December

b) *Days of the week* (i giorni della settimana)

lunedì	Monday
martedì	Tuesday
mercoledì	Wednesday
giovedì	Thursday
venerdì	Friday
sabato	Saturday
domenica *(feminine)*	Sunday

c) *Seasons* (le stagioni)

la primavera	spring
l'estate *(feminine)*	summer
l'autunno	autumn
l'inverno	winter

For prepositions used with the seasons see p 230.

Note that all Italian months, days and seasons are masculine except for la domenica and l'estate, and they do not take a capital letter.

2 Dates

a) Cardinal numbers (eg due, tre) are used for the days of the month except for the first:

	il ventun marzo	**l'otto giugno**
	the twenty-first of March	the eighth of June
But:	**il primo luglio**	
	the first of July	

The definite article is used but prepositions (eg of, on) are generally omitted:

sono nata il ventotto aprile 1985
I was born on 28 April, 1985

ti ho scritto il sei (di) ottobre
I wrote to you on the sixth of October

b) The year is expressed by the full cardinal number (or by the last two figures of it), preceded by the definite article or by the day and the month. Of course, in writing, the numeral and not the word is normally used:

il millenovecentonovantadue   **il novantadue**
1992   '92

sono nato nel 1988
I was born in 1988

c) 'Today' is expressed as follows:

che giorno è oggi?   **oggi è Sabato**
what day is it today?   today is Saturday

quanti ne abbiamo oggi?   **oggi ne abbiamo tre**
what is the date today?   today is the third

che giorno è oggi?   **oggi è il 3 (tre) giugno**
what is the date today?   today is 3rd June

oggi è giovedì 5 (cinque) aprile
today is Thursday, 5th April

3 Age

Age is usually expressed by the verb avere + number + anni:

quanti anni hai?   **ha trentadue anni**
how old are you?   he/she is thirty-two

che età ha?   **a che età ...?**
what age is he/she/are you?   at what age ...?

una donna di quarant'anni
a forty-year-old woman

all'età di diciotto anni si diventa maggiorenni
one comes of age at eighteen

un uomo sui quarant'anni/sulla quarantina
a man of about forty

C USEFUL EXPRESSIONS

sono le sei passate	it is past 6 o'clock
alle quattro precise/in punto	at exactly 4 o'clock
verso le nove	about 9 o'clock
verso mezzanotte	about midnight
sono appena suonate le nove	it has just struck nine
allo scoccare delle tre	on the stroke of three
dalle 9 in poi/a partire dalle 9	from 9 o'clock onwards
poco prima delle sette	shortly before seven
poco dopo le sette	shortly after seven
prima o poi	sooner or later
il più presto possibile	as soon as possible
il più tardi possibile	as late as possible
al più presto	at the earliest
al più tardi	at the latest
è tardi/presto	it is late/early
sei in ritardo/anticipo	you are late/early
mi alzo tardi	I get up late
è arrivato in ritardo	he arrived late
il treno ha venti minuti di ritardo	the train is twenty minutes late
il mio orologio è indietro di sei minuti	my watch is six minutes slow
il mio orologio è avanti di sei minuti	my watch is six minutes fast
oggi, ieri, domani	today, yesterday, tomorrow
l'altro ieri	the day before yesterday
dopodomani	the day after tomorrow
l'indomani	the next day
tre giorni fa	three days ago

fra tre giorni	in three days' time
questa settimana	this week
la settimana scorsa	last week
oggi a otto	today week, a week today
quindici giorni	a fortnight
stamattina	this morning
ieri mattina	yesterday morning
domattina, domani mattina	tomorrow morning
oggi pomeriggio	this afternoon
ieri pomeriggio	yesterday afternoon
domani pomeriggio	tomorrow afternoon
stasera	this evening, tonight
ieri sera	yesterday evening, last night
domani sera	tomorrow night
stanotte	tonight, last night
lunedì	on Monday
di lunedì, il lunedì, al lunedì	on Mondays
ogni lunedì, tutti i lunedì	every Monday
un'oretta	about an hour
una mezz'ora	a half-hour, half an hour
una mezz'oretta	about half an hour
un quarto d'ora	a quarter of an hour
tre quarti d'ora	three quarters of an hour
passare il tempo (a fare)	to spend one's time (doing)
perdere tempo	to waste time
di tanto in tanto	from time to time
nel 2001	in 2001
negli anni Venti/Trenta	in the Twenties/Thirties
negli anni '20	in the 20s
nel Duemila	in the 21st century
nel XX (ventesimo) secolo	in the 20th century
un piano quinquennale	a five-year plan
un anno bisestile	a leap year
un anno civile	a calendar year
un anno luce	a light year

11 THE SENTENCE

A WORD ORDER

Word order is usually broadly the same in Italian as in English, except in the following cases:

1 Adjectives

Many Italian adjectives follow the noun (*see* pp 54-7):

una ragazza italiana
an *Italian* girl

hai gli ochi azzurri
you have *blue* eyes

2 Adverbs

In simple tenses, adverbs usually follow the verb (*see* pp 73-4):

ci vado spesso
I *often* go there

farà buio presto
it will *soon* be dark

3 Object pronouns

Unstressed object pronouns usually come before the verb (*see* pp 81-2):

ti aspetterò
I'll wait for *you*

gliel'ha venduto
he/she sold *it* to *him/her/them/you*

4 Noun phrases

Noun phrases are formed differently in Italian (*see* p 266):

una camicia di cotone
a cotton shirt

il padre del mio amico
my friend's father

5 Exclamations

The word order is not affected after come, che and quanto (used as an adjective) which are usually followed by an adjective or noun:

come fa freddo!
it's so cold!

come canta male!
he/she sings so badly!

quanti fiori!
what a lot of flowers!

che aria stanca aveva!
he/she looked so tired!

quante stupidaggini hai detto!
what a lot of silly things you said!

che brutto è stato quel viaggio!
what an awful journey that was!

6 Verbs of motion

The normal word order with verbs of motion is verb first followed by the subject:

sta arrivando Giovanni
Giovanni is coming

è venuta mia mamma
my mum has come

7 Emphasis

Italian word order is usually very flexible. A different word order can convey a shift in emphasis, something that in English would often be achieved by a change in intonation. As a general rule, the emphasis in an Italian sentence lies on the last word:

Pietro me l'ha dato
Pietro gave it to me

me l'ha dato Pietro
Pietro gave it to me

B NEGATIVE EXPRESSIONS

1 Principal negative words

no	no
non	not

non ... più	no more/longer, not ... any more/any longer
non ... mai	never, not ... ever
non ... nulla	nothing, not ... anything
non ... niente	nothing, not ... anything
non ... nessuno	no one, nobody, not ... anybody
non ... nessuno	not ... any, no
non ... alcuno	not ... any, no
non ... affatto	not ... at all
non ... mica	not ... at all
non ... per niente	not ... at all
non ... neanche	not ... even
non ... neppure	not ... even
non ... nemmeno	not ... even
non ... né ... né	neither ... nor
non ... che	only ...

Note that non ... che (only) is less common than solo, solamente, soltanto (only):

non c'è che mio padre che mi capisce
only my father understands me

2 Position of negative expressions

a) *With simple tenses, the infinitive and the imperative*

Negative words enclose the verb: non comes before the verb and the other negative element comes after the verb:

non dire niente!
don't say anything!

non lo ripetere mai!
never mention this to anyone!

non mi piace per niente
I don't like it at all

non mangiate più!
don't eat any more!

non è affatto vero
it's not true at all

qui non c'è nessuno
there's no one here

su questo non c'è nessun dubbio
there's no doubt about this

non è né nero né grigio
it's neither black nor grey

preferiamo non vedere nessuno
we prefer not to see anyone

ha giurato di non perdonarlo mai
he/she swore never to forgive him

non lo vogliono nemmeno vedere
they don't even want to see him

non è mica male!
it's not bad at all

b) *With compound tenses*

   i) in the case of non ... più, mai, affatto, mica, neanche, nemmeno
      and neppure, non precedes the auxiliary but the second negative
      element may either precede or follow the past participle:

      non è più tornata/non è tornata più
      she never came back

      non l'ho neppure visto/non l'ho visto neppure
      I didn't even see him

      non li abbiamo nemmeno letti/non li abbiamo letti nemmeno
      we haven't even read them

   ii) in the case of non ... nulla, niente, nessuno and per niente, the
       second negative element follows the past participle:

       non gli abbiamo promesso niente
       we didn't promise him/them anything

       non abbiamo invitato nessuno
       we haven't invited anybody

c) *At the beginning of the sentence*

   When nessuno, mai, niente *etc* are placed at the beginning of the
   sentence non is omitted:

   nessuno lo sospetta
   no one suspects it

   né Caterina né Pino sono venuti
   neither Caterina nor Pino has come

   nulla è cambiato
   nothing has changed

3 Combinations of negative expressions

Negative expressions may be combined as follows:

> non ... mai più   non ... mai niente   non ... mai nessuno
> non ... più niente/nulla   non ... più nessuno

non ci vedremo mai più
we shall never see each other again

non c'è più niente da fare
there's nothing left to be done

non ha mai niente da dire, lui
he never has anything to say

non vedi mai nessuno
you never see anyone

dopo di te non posso più amare nessuno
after you I can't love anybody again

4 Negative expressions without a verb

a) non

ti piace? – non molto
do you like it? – not much

lo vedi spesso? – no, non tanto
do you see him often? – no, not really

b) no

Note in particular the following uses of no:

tu ci vai? – io no!
are you going? – no, I'm not!

a te piace? – a me no!
do you like it? – no, I don't!

un giorno sì e uno no
every other day

vieni sì o no?
are you coming or not?

credo di no
I don't think so

c) niente affatto

ti piace? – niente affatto!
do you like it? – no way!

d) nemmeno

noi non ci vogliamo andare – nemmeno io!
we don't want to go – neither do I!

non abbiamo mangiato nulla – nemmeno noi
we haven't eaten anything – neither have we

e) mai più

tornerai a Hull? – mai più
will you ever come back to Hull? – no, never

tornerai al lunapark? – mai più!
are you going back to the fair? – never again!

C DIRECT AND INDIRECT QUESTIONS

1 Direct questions

There are two main ways of forming direct questions in Italian:

❑ by inflection of the voice: subject + verb
❑ by inversion: (question word) + verb + subject

a) *Inflection*

The word order remains the same as in statements (subject + verb) but the intonation changes: the voice is raised at the end of the sentence. This is the most common question form in Italian:

parli italiano?
do you speak Italian?

ti piace?
(do) you like it?

sono arrivati stamattina?
did they arrive this morning?

la pasta fa ingrassare?
is pasta fattening?

Gabriele ha scritto alla nonna?
has Gabriele written to his grandma?

b) *Inversion*

> **si è divertito il tuo amico?**
> did your friend have a good time?

> **splende il sole da voi?**
> is the sun shining where you are?

This is the normal form when a question word is used:

> **cosa sta mangiando Paolo?**
> what is Paolo eating?

Note that with the verb 'to be' the word order in Italian is slightly different from English, as the subject can be placed only at the beginning or at the end of the sentence:

> **Giovanni è studioso?**
> **è studioso Giovanni?**
> is Giovanni hard-working?

2 Indirect questions

a) *Word order*

Indirect questions can be introduced either by question words (like come, perché, che cosa *etc*) or by the conjunction se 'whether/ if'. The word order is usually the same as in direct questions, with or without inversion:

direct	*indirect*
come ti chiami?	**dimmi come ti chiami**
what is your name?	tell me what your name is

direct	*indirect*
le piace il caffè	**mi dica se le piace il caffè**
do you like coffee?	tell me whether you like coffee

b) Indirect questions may be introduced by chiedere or domandare (to ask). Particular attention should be paid to the sequence of tenses:

> **Simona mi chiede se ho freddo** *(present)*
> Simona is asking me if I am cold

mi chiese/mi ha chiesto se stavo bene *(imperfect)*
he/she asked me if I was well

domandò loro se avevano visto suo figlio *(pluperfect)*
he/she asked them if they had seen his/her son

Marco ha chiesto a Delia se sarebbe andata in biblioteca *(past conditional)*
Marco asked Delia if she would be going to the library

Note the following points:

i) In the last example English uses the present conditional but Italian must use the past conditional in an indirect question since the verb in the main clause is in the past tense. The same is true of any indirect sentence:

   disse che avrebbe voluto ammazzarlo
   he/she said he/she would like to kill him

ii) The subjunctive may be used in place of the indicative in the subordinate clause particularly in more formal or literary Italian:

   domandò loro se avessero visto suo figlio
   he/she asked them if they had seen his/her son

   Gianni le chiese dove andasse
   Gianni asked her where she was going

3 Translation of English question tags

Examples of question tags are: isn't it?, aren't you?, doesn't he?, won't they?, haven't you?, is it?, did you? *etc.* Question tags are not used in Italian as often as they are in English. Some of them can, however, be translated in the following ways:

i) by placing **vero, è vero, non è vero, no** at the end of the sentence:
   è molto simpatica, vero?   **la pizza piace a tutti, no?**
   she's very nice, isn't she?   everyone likes pizza, don't they?

ii) by placing **è vero che** at the beginning of the sentence:
   è vero che vorresti venire con noi?
   you'd like to come with us, wouldn't you?

4 Answers ('yes' and 'no')

a) sì means 'yes' and is also equivalent to longer positive answers such as 'yes, it is', 'yes, I will', 'yes, he has' *etc*. It can be reinforced by certo or certamente:

mi scriverai? – sì, certo!
will you write to me? – (yes) of course I will

b) no means 'no' and is also equivalent to longer negative answers such as: 'no, it isn't', 'no, I didn't' *etc*:

è andato bene l'esame? – no, ho fatto un sacco di errori
did the exam go well? – no (it didn't), I made a lot of mistakes

12 TRANSLATION PROBLEMS

1 False friends

A considerable number of words which appear to be recognizable through English in fact have (or may have) a different meaning in Italian:

abusivo	unauthorized, unlawful (**ingiurioso** = abusive)
assistere	to attend (as well as 'to assist')
attuale	present, topical (**reale** = actual)
coincidenza	connection (in transport)
combinazione	coincidence
disgrazia	misfortune, trouble (as well as 'disgrace')
editore	publisher (**redattore** = newspaper editor)
energetico	energy (**la crisi energetica** = the energy crisis)
energico	energetic
incidente	accident
manifestazione	demonstration, event
novella	short story (**romanzo** = novel)
palazzo	block of flats (but also 'palace')
pavimento	floor (**marciapiede** = pavement)
petrolio	oil (**benzina** = petrol)
sensibile	sensitive (**sensato** = sensible)
tempestivo	timely (**tempestoso** = stormy)
ultimamente	recently (**infine** = ultimately)
visita	examination, inspection (as well as 'visit')

2 Foreign borrowings in Italian

Some words may be immediately recognizable such as **sport**, **leader** or **meeting**. Some may have been translated literally into Italian, for instance **pioggia acida** (acid rain) and **effetto serra** (greenhouse effect). In some cases, however, although the word seems to be a direct borrowing, the meaning has in fact shifted: **un night** (a night-club), **un toast** (a toasted sandwich), **un golf** (a cardigan or sweater). Sometimes both English and Italian will have borrowed from another language, eg **un colpo di stato** (a coup d'état).

3 Problems associated with parts of speech

The following sections correspond broadly to the earlier chapters in the book and should be studied in conjunction with them:

a) *Definite article*

The definite article may be obligatory in Italian but not in English. Do not feel obliged to retain it just because it is in the original:

la Scozia	**non mangia la carne**
Scotland	he/she doesn't eat meat
i vini italiani sono buoni	**il coraggio è una buona qualità**
Italian wines are good	courage is a good quality
l'estate è più calda della primavera	
summer is hotter than spring	

b) *Partitive*

This may be translated as *some* or *any* in English but it may also be omitted:

ho comprato del salame	**vuoi del pane?**
I've bought some salami	do you want any/some bread?
ha degli amici a Rimini	
he/she has friends in Rimini	

c) *Genitive*

la macchina di mia zia
my aunt's car

i mariti delle mie colleghe
my colleagues' husbands

sai l'indirizzo del capo di mio padre?
do you know my father's boss's address?
do you know the address of my father's boss?

la politica estera del governo britannico
the British government's foreign policy
the foreign policy of the British government

d) *Nouns*

i) singulars and plurals:
Italian habitually uses a singular in the following type of sentence:

si sono tolti il cappotto
they took off their coats

hanno messo la cartella sulla scrivania
they put their briefcases on the desk/on their desks

Some words are normally plural in Italian, however, and singular in English:

ha fatto dei notevoli progressi
he/she has made great progress

ho chiesto delle informazioni
I asked for information

But remember to be consistent if a pronoun is used:

le ho chieste *(le informazioni)*
I asked for it

A singular form does exist in some cases but it must be translated slightly differently:

un'informazione	**una notizia**	**un mobile**
a piece of information	an item of news	a piece of furniture

ii) gender:

A masculine plural noun may mask a mixture of male and female: **i figli** may mean 'sons' but it may also mean 'children'.

A feminine plural noun may have to have some indication of gender added in English if it is not otherwise clear from the context:

le mie allieve
my female pupils

iii) suffixes:

These should be translated in English by using one or even two adjectives:

una vecchietta
a little old lady
una giornataccia
a really bad day
un chiacchierone
a chatterbox

una bella casetta
a nice little house
un librone
a big thick book

iv) noun phrases:

A noun phrase consists of two nouns used in combination. English requires no connecting preposition and the order of the nouns is reversed:

un corso d'aggiornamento
a refresher course
le previsioni del tempo
the weather forecast
il codice della strada
the highway code
una crisi di governo
a government crisis
i libri di testo
text books

una polizza d'assicurazione
an insurance policy
uno sciopero della fame
a hunger strike
una patente di guida
a driving licence
il treno delle otto
the eight o'clock train

e) *Adjectives*

The translation of adjectives into English often involves changes in word order:

un vestito azzurro
a light-blue dress

un ragazzo piccolo e magro
a thin little boy

un giovane artista promettente
a promising young artist

la vita istituzionale e politica italiana
Italian political and institutional life

un ambiente comodo, piacevole, accogliente
a comfortable, pleasant and welcoming environment

Note that in lists of either nouns or adjectives English adds 'and' between the last two elements, whereas in Italian this is not required.

Note

Certain Italian adjectives may change their meaning according to whether they precede or follow the noun:

uno studente povero
a poor student
(not well-off)

un povero studente
a poor student
(unfortunate)

---

f) *Pronouns*

i) subject and object pronouns:
The former are frequently omitted in Italian:

ha lavorato sodo
he/she has worked hard/you have worked hard *(polite form)*

è sul tavolo
it's on the table

The Italian neuter pronoun lo is frequently omitted in translation:

è chiuso, non lo sapevi?
it's closed, didn't you know?

ii) pleonastic pronouns:

Particularly in the spoken language, a pronoun may be used even if the noun to which it corresponds is also present in the sentence. It will normally be omitted in English:

la pera l'ho già mangiata   **tu ce l'hai la macchina?**
I've already eaten the pear   have you got the/a car?

iii) ne

The particle ne (some, any, some of it, some of them *etc*)   is often not translated in English:

ne hai a casa? – sì, ne ho tre
have you got any/some at home? – yes, I've got three

iv) si

Care must be taken with the translation of the pronoun si as it has a number of uses in Italian – as a reflexive, a reflexive of reciprocity, in passive constructions, and as an impersonal pronoun (remember that sì meaning 'yes' always has an accent):

si va avanti?   **si deve tagliare così**
shall we carry on?   you have to cut it like this

ci si sente terribilmente soli   **si dice che ha torto**
one feels awfully alone   they/people say he's/she's wrong

non si vedono spesso gli scoiattoli
you don't often see squirrels

v) se

It is important not to confuse se meaning 'if' with the pronoun:

se si vedono spesso, litigano
if they see each other often, they quarrel

se lo dice ogni tanto
he/she says that every so often

vi) possessives:

These are used far more often in English than in Italian and must frequently be added in translation, particularly with parts of the body and items of clothing:

dammi la mano
give me your hand

ha infilato i pantaloni
he/she put on his/her trousers

il vestito era nuovo fiammante
his suit was brand new

una madre coi figli
a mother with her children

vii) relative pronouns

These cannot be omitted in Italian (as they frequently are in English):

il disco che ho comprato
the record (that/which) I bought

l'uomo con cui parlavo
the man (who/that) I was speaking to

g) *Verbs*

It is vital to recognize the tenses and persons of verbs. Irregular verbs have traditionally been the cause of most problems but even regular ones can occasionally be 'misread'. Examples include finirono (they finished) and finiranno (they will finish), andremo (we shall go) and andremmo (we would go), mi fermai (I stopped) and mi fermerai (you will stop me).

A single tense form in Italian may give rise to a number of possible translations in English according to the context:

andavo al cinema
I was going to the cinema
I used to go/would go to the
    cinema

tornerà l'anno prossimo
he will come back next year
he is coming back next year
he will be (coming) back next year
he is going to come back next year

A verb such as fare is used in a very wide range of expressions in Italian and may need to be translated by many different English verbs, for example:

fa caldo
it's hot

non ho fatto attenzione
I didn't pay attention

facciamo una passeggiata
let's go for a walk

hanno fatto una domanda
they asked a question

ho fatto un bagno
I had a bath

mi fece compagnia
he/she kept me company

h) *Sequence of tenses*

Special care must be taken with some typically Italian tense sequences which differ from English:

i) with da meaning 'since':

da quanto siete sposati? *(present)*
how long have you been married for?

è da molto che non ti vedo *(present)*
I haven't seen you for ages

aspettavo da ore *(imperfect)*
I had been waiting for hours

ii) with a past conditional:

sapevo che sarebbe finita così
I knew it would end up like this

pensavo che ormai l'argomento sarebbe stato chiuso
I thought the subject would be closed by now

i) *Prepositions*

Direct equivalence cannot always be expected between Italian and English prepositions as the following examples with da (from, by) indicate:

l'uomo dai capelli scuri
the man with the dark hair

da un lato ... dall'altro
on the one hand ... on the other

da che il mondo è mondo
ever since the world began

vado dal macellaio
I'm going to the butcher's

4 Idioms

Both Italian and English are rich in idiomatic expressions. Where possible you should try to match an Italian idiom with an equivalent English one, but if this is not possible the meaning must be expressed in a non-idiomatic way. Remember that some idioms are more colloquial than others and may not be appropriate for the context:

pioveva a catinelle
it was bucketing down

tagliamo la corda!
let's get out of here!

sono al verde!
I'm broke!

detto fatto
no sooner said than done

fare una vita da cani
to lead a dog's life

ha troppa carne al fuoco
he has too many irons in the fire

questo è un altro paio di maniche
that's another kettle of fish

si è ridotta una straccia
she was a shadow of her former self

sono rimasta male
I was taken aback

sono fritto!
now I've had it!

l'ho piantato in asso
I left him in the lurch

fumare come un turco
to smoke like a chimney

menare il can per l'aia
to beat about the bush

pallido/bianco come un cencio
as white as a sheet

5 Proper nouns

First names should not normally be translated into English even where an English equivalent exists (an exception is made for names of popes and kings and so on). With the names of Italian towns, islands and so on, on the other hand, where an English version exists, it should be used:

Firenze	Florence	**Sardegna**	Sardinia
Genova	Genoa	**Torino**	Turin
Milano	Milan	**Venezia**	Venice
Padova	Padua		

Similarly, Italian versions of foreign names should be translated:

Ginevra	Geneva	**Mosca**	Moscow
Londra	London	**Parigi**	Paris

Street names should be left in Italian:

abitano in via Santo Spirito 15
they live at 15, via Santo Spirito

INDEX

273